LEADERSHIP STYLE

BUSINESS AND LEADERSHIP IN CHINA

LEADERSHIP STYLE

BUSINESS AND LEADERSHIP IN CHINA

Editors

Pedro Nueno
Xiaoming Zhu

CEIBS, China

Translated by

Weng Wei • Xiao Yang

World Scientific

NEW JERSEY • LONDON • SINGAPORE • BEIJING • SHANGHAI • HONG KONG • TAIPEI • CHENNAI • TOKYO

Published by

World Scientific Publishing Co. Pte. Ltd.
5 Toh Tuck Link, Singapore 596224
USA office: 27 Warren Street, Suite 401-402, Hackensack, NJ 07601
UK office: 57 Shelton Street, Covent Garden, London WC2H 9HE

Library of Congress Cataloging-in-Publication Data
Names: Nueno Iniesta, Pedro, editor. | Zhu, Xiaoming (Professor of management), editor. | Wei, Weng, translator. | Yang, Xiao (Translator), translator.
Title: Leadership style : business and leadership in China / editors, Pedro Nueno, Xiaoming Zhu, CEIBS, China ; translated by Weng Wei, Xiao Yang.
Other titles: 880-01 Ling dao fan er. English
Description: Singapore ; Hackensack, NJ : World Scientific, [2020] | "Originally published in Chinese by Fudan University Press, Copyright licensed by Fudan University Press and arranged with Shanghai CEIBS Online Learning Co. Ltd., 2011"-- Title page verso.
Identifiers: LCCN 2020010784 | ISBN 9789813275256 (hardcover) | ISBN 9789813275263 (ebook) | ISBN 9789813275270 (ebook other)
Subjects: LCSH: Leadership--China.
Classification: LCC HD57.7 .L56213 2020 | DDC 658.4/0920951--dc23
LC record available at https://lccn.loc.gov/2020010784

British Library Cataloguing-in-Publication Data
A catalogue record for this book is available from the British Library.

《领导范儿》
Originally published in Chinese by Fudan University Press
Copyright licensed by Fudan University Press and arranged with
Shanghai CEIBS Online Learning Co. Ltd., 2011

For any available supplementary material, please visit
https://www.worldscientific.com/worldscibooks/10.1142/11129#t=suppl

Desk Editor: Ong Shi Min Nicole

Typeset by Stallion Press
Email: enquiries@stallionpress.com

Preface

Continuous Learning for Sustainable Development

It is the best time. It is also the most trying time for people to show wisdom.

Chinese enterprises have never been faced with such a broad stage for development as they are now. Today, they have been faced with vigorously-growing business opportunities. With plenty of entrepreneurial experiences, Chinese enterprises have a strong desire for growth. Meanwhile, the market is changing more rapidly than ever before. Disruptive innovations emerge in an endless stream, spurred by diverse external forces, new technologies and new business models. A variety of black swan events interlocked with multiple positive forces demonstrate association crossing time and space.

Having braved the wind and waves for 30 years since the policy of reform and opening-up, the Chinese ship of entrepreneurism finally sails into the endless sea. The voice ringing in entrepreneurs' ears will no longer be the gibbons' howls on both banks of the river, but the muffled cries of whales in the ocean. Looking back on the past 30 years, Chinese enterprises have been fearless, daring, and courageous. In the meantime, they have also embraced great learning ability and entrepreneurship cultivated by the thousands-year-old Eastern culture, such as "There must be one out of three who can be your teacher", and "Western learning spreads to the east". It is this daring and learning ability that has helped Chinese enterprises to renew and develop Chinese entrepreneurship and business traditions that have been discontinued for decades.

Compared with those powerful international companies with long histories and great strength, daring and learning ability will be important competitive advantages for Chinese companies that have fallen behind in terms of technology and management. In turn, it is necessary for a great deal of foreign multinationals to thoroughly study the Chinese way of doing business and localize themselves so as to fully tap on the huge Chinese market. We believe that this serves as an important driving force for the vigorous development of Chinese business schools that have sprung up during the past decade. This is also a critical foundation for CEIBS to continuously create miracles during the past 17 years since its establishment.

CEIBS is committed to continuous learning and constant improvement of Chinese enterprises. Since 2001, the school's MBA and EMBA educational programmes have ranked at the top of the list across the Asia-Pacific area for many years, crowding into the first-class schools around the world. CEIBS is also home to EQUIS and AACSB, two of the most famous international certifications for business schools. Chinese former Premier Wen Jiabao spoke of CEIBS as the cradle of a large number of outstanding managers.

It is not our desire that the education model in business school only encourages people to study at a fixed time and location, which cannot satisfy the enterprises' requirements for talents. What CEIBS advocates is "lifelong and continuous learning". People speak highly of General Electric (GE) in the era of Jack Welch. How did GE, under Welch, achieve a world-known success? During the 20 years when Welch had been at the helm, GE suffered a good many hardships and risks, but the company kept growing. One of the secrets, in the words of Welch, is that "(they) are learning every day," and "hope (their) employees have enthusiasm for finding a better way every morning they wake up, and seek the enthusiasm from colleagues in the workplace and other companies...".

In May 2008, we launched the first issue of *CEIBS Business Review*, a monthly magazine, aiming at bringing the wisdom and research of CEIBS to enterprises so as to help entrepreneurs and senior managers deal with the changing business environment, reflect on their business's strengths and shortcomings, and break through management bottlenecks to improve leadership. In this sense, *CEIBS Business Review* can be considered as a "mobile" business school that is always around the businessmen in their daily management lives.

As a stratagem, this "mobile" business school will adhere to the philosophy of "Demonstrating Depth of China and Breadth across the Globe" proposed by CEIBS. With a commitment to becoming a must-read for senior managers in the decision-making process, this book will help companies to make the right decisions from multiple dimensions, including corporate environment, internal management, and personal leadership.

In the three years since *CEIBS Business Review* was first published, its editorial team, trying its best with all sincerity and professionalism, has been dedicated to making the magazine a top publication in the field of business management in China. The magazine enjoys unique teacher resources, such as Wu Jinglian, Xu Xiaonian, Yang Guoan, Ding Yuan, Li Xiujuan, and unique research resources, such as the Central European Lujiazui International Finance Research Institute, Case Research Center, Private Enterprise Research Center, Entrepreneurship Center, Human Resources and Organization Management Research Center. These resources have shown continuous care and help for the magazine to convey authoritative opinions and research results to readers.

Compared with other business or management magazines, *CEIBS Business Review* displays its unique personality in three aspects. The first one is to focus on the management and leadership of Chinese enterprises; the second one is to make an extensive and in-depth study of the practices of Chinese companies to condense original management thoughts; the third one is to continuously disseminate international advanced management concepts and models. At the same time, the magazine also makes unremitting efforts to improve text readability with fresh cases.

During the past three years, the magazine has accumulated a large number of thoughtful articles with long-term significance. We have reorganized them into different categories, and published the articles in the form of *CEIBS Business Review collections*. These collections will be launched one after another to facilitate more readers who can make great progress through continuous learning.

As an old Chinese saying goes, "A diligent learner is like the seedling planted in spring; it usually doesn't seem to get taller, but it grows every day. A sluggish learner is like the stone used to sharpen knives; it usually doesn't seem to get smaller, but it is thinned every day." We believe that a company that continues to learn for self-improvement can thrive in adversity and break through the winter ice like spring seedlings. On the contrary, companies would still languish even if the economic crisis did not exist.

There is no limit to the business world. We hope that Chinese entrepreneurs will embrace a brighter future with a development-oriented learning attitude!

Zhu Xiaoming
Chinese President and Professor of Management at CEIBS

Pedro Nueno
European President and Professor of Entrepreneurship at CEIBS
April 2011

Foreword

Innovating Management for Future Success

Three years ago in May, a magazine was born. With a calm, professional, personal, sincere and elegant temperament, the magazine kept quiet in the noisy world, even though it was standing on the shoulders of the giants.

Three years later, its quiet power spreads in the Chinese business community like the inexorable life force when it was born in the spring. Of course, its circulation does not rely on suffocating cries, nor forced and wronged promotion. Instead, it is based on a sense of community between the publication and business circles, the common determination to strive for a brighter future, a warm handshake between theory and practice through in-depth research, and its unique temperament from the inside out.

Three years is but a moment in the long history of Chinese enterprises. However, these three years have brought together more sorrows and glories than one can imagine, such as the Wenchuan Earthquake, Japan's nuclear leak, the Olympic Games, the World Expo, financial tsunami, and wars in North Africa. In the midst of such an extreme environment, Chinese companies are constantly dispelling the clouds and intensively striving for growth.

One wild bump after another during these three years have made us realise that currently the dividend of public system innovation has been marginally reduced to an almost stagnant level, and the number of institutional opportunities has also fallen. The "economy of social connection" and "daring companies" will exit from the mainstream, and market-discovering companies will surely move toward market-innovative businesses. The fundamentals of promoting product innovation, R&D innovation, business model innovation, and market innovation will be increasingly tied to the ability to manage organizations.

Such a change of mindset and transfer of ability lay the foundation and created the value of this magazine. Relying on the abundant wisdom and research capacity of China Europe International Business School (CEIBS), we turn our focus to the actual operation of companies. We are concerned about the companies' concerns and the difficulties of managing a business. By summarizing lessons and crystallizing advanced and innovative theories, we aim to present a pragmatic and realistic growth map.

Looking back, our efforts still have timeless practical significance, or even more prominence in today's business world, some of which will be shown as followed.

In July 2008, we took the lead in proposing the concept of "knowledge-intensive enterprise" after thoroughly investigating the Huawei model in the third issue of *CEIBS Business Review*. By studying Huawei's ways of management, we find out that though these enterprises are in the category of "labor-intensive" companies, they are different in certain ways. That is because their "labors" are "knowledge labors" that can create high additional value so as to become the driving forces for innovation due to the low-cost "labor-intensive" combined with high value-added "knowledge".

In the fourth issue, we acted as a pioneer in promoting the "low carbon strategy" as a cover story to help companies think about how to avoid risks and utilize opportunities more than a year before the Copenhagen Climate Conference, when many Chinese companies did not pay enough attention to this issue. Today, the significance of these articles is highlighted.

In July 2009, when the C2C market was still in full swing, we first proposed "the maturity of B2C market" in China. In addition to predicting that the B2C market would surpass the C2C market to become the mainstream of e-commerce, we also conducted in-depth research into how B2C enterprises need to focus on supply chain as a priority, and how traditional enterprises balance online and offline business.

In September 2009, we extended our reach into company politics that people often avoid. Do company politics have to be avoided or unchecked? Are company politics always the bad kid who destroys corporate culture? This is not the case. We proposed the concept of incorporating company politics into management. Company politics cannot be avoided, and if managed well, it can be a track to guide companies into healthy competition and interaction.

In March 2010, we systematically studied the mysteries behind decision-making, revealing a variety of "implicit rules for decision-making" that have a major or minor impact on companies. In fact, the implicit rules "are not reasons, but personalities and emotions", which makes it important for decision-makers to keep sober and alert. Thus, how should the best decision be made?

In October 2010, we put our perspective of discovery into the field of "state-business relations" that are often difficult to deal with, but which companies still have to face. If we regard the previously distorted, short-sighted, high-risk state-business relations as the 1.0 era, then a new, healthy and long-lasting state-business relationship is the 2.0 era. This new type of relationship is based on the respective characteristics and needs of state and business in the modern law-ruled society, in pursuit of a relationship characterized by positive interaction, win-win cooperation, and mutual development to benefit the whole society. It can help participants in the market re-recognize fundamental inner demands. So, how should companies develop this relationship? How can entrepreneurs and officials maintain a safe distance to avoid risks?

In 2011, we launched "The People Around the Boss" in the January issue to study the relationship between the aides of the people in charge and corporate decisions, and the way to be a good aide. This has practical guidance for companies that have adopted an extensive mode of decision-making and development, and for corporate executives who experience the ups and downs of the business world every day.

In March 2011, we proposed the concept of "purchasing myself" through systematic research to reveal the relationship between "things" and "people" in marketing. According to this concept, in addition to consuming a commodity's properties and functions, consumers make purchase decisions to satisfy the needs of self-determination and self-manifestation by buying emotions, psychology, values, and ideas attached to commodities. "Buying myself" means consuming oneself, which is a process of self-release. Sellers can plan a specific emotional tipping point to encourage customers to awaken or arouse themselves.

In addition, we also explored how China's manufacturing industry launched the "third industrial revolution", how to make good use of "foreign talents" in the increasingly fierce international competition, how business management transformed from extensive mode into the normalized enterprise management mode through in-depth research on The Creative Life Corporation (TCL), how to regain momentum for China's first-class enterprises, how to carry out marketing activities in the YOU era, how to build "Heartfelt Leadership", how to make "wetware" to promote innovation, how to enter the era of "Legalization Survives", how the new bizarre platform-type enterprises rose and influenced the world, the difference between elite entrepreneurship and grassroots entrepreneurship, how blue-collar management evolved, how entrepreneurs gained a deep sense of happiness, how to manage the new generation of "reactionary" groups, and so on. By studying and exploring the management challenges facing Chinese companies, we have brought innovation into management step by step.

Along the way, as seasons come and seasons go, we have continuously bowed our heads to explore, and thought carefully to deliver rigorous articles during the more than 1,000 days. We have attempted to understand the pains and gains of Chinese companies, hoping to cater to their needs. Without being complacent, we try to work diligently to pool together the wisdom of all parties and deliver the professional ideas and thoughts in the forms of readable columns of "new management", "incisive management", "fun management" to satisfy the underlying needs of companies.

Meanwhile, we feel delighted and more confident to see every inspiration and innovation, success, and progress of Chinese companies. What makes us more ambitious, as a 3-year-old "kid", we have received generous help from management gurus at home and abroad, including Peter Senge, James Champy, Charles Handy, Hermann Simon, John Naisbitt, Wu Jinglian, Yang Guoan, Hu Yong, and Chen Chunhua. These gurus and many outstanding entrepreneurs have strengthened our belief that every word we delivered has great value in the impetuous society. Such values will make necessary, realistic, and inevitable contributions to the sustainable growth of Chinese enterprises, the flourishing of a class of men, and the continuous evolution of our society.

On the third anniversary of the magazine's publication, we have sorted through more than 1,300 articles that were carefully written and polished, especially those with lingering effects, and have reorganized the articles in the form of the *CEIBS Business Review* collection. The ageless thoughts stemming from practice are no longer confined to the limitations of a monthly publishing format, which can be shown to the readers at all times for reading, learning and criticizing.

At the same time, the reprint in the form of a collection also contains our gratefulness for the continued support of the magazine publishers, CEBIS and Shanghai Yuan Dong Publishing House, for the constant research and compositions from academic and business writers. We also give our thanks to people who provide various help and give a smile to us, including you, our dear readers.

Our series will be divided into different categories, such as leadership, humanism, marketing, cover stories, cases, which will be launched one after another soon.

Zhou Xuelin
Publisher of *CEIBS Business Review* and Assistant Dean of CEIBS

Li Mingwei
Executive Editor of CEIBS
April 2011

Contents

Whether you're leading a business or a non-profit organization, a committee or a board, an athletic team or a family, you must learn when to compromise and when to stand firm. Although it's not possible to resolve every conflict through negotiation and concession, it is feasible in most cases.

Since kindergarten, people have been taught to resolve problems using top-down rules, listen to authoritative opinions and ignore their own thoughts, avoid self-expression beyond requirement as it can cause trouble; stay within the scope of duties as it is the safest way.... However, they are all old-fashioned ideas that need to be shattered by Liberating Leaders whose mission is to create freedom-form organizations.

Sometimes it is hard to define "decent work". 20 years ago, the best students in China chose to major in electrical automation; 10 years ago, the first choice of the top students in high school was often life science; today, economics and management majors are the most sought-after. So the "decent work" chosen by teenagers who have just begun to design their life according to social trends has undergone several rounds of change, which can be explained by the lyrics of Faye Wong: "Nothing will last forever."

Not all top managers are qualified to launch a major reform. Their position will be changed if they fail to change their minds. Nor is every reformer qualified to give an impassioned speech easily. To achieve the final success of reforms, reformers need to have motives that truly represent the core objectives of the organization and reflect the underlying needs of the majority of members in the organization. Managers should be able to formulate appropriate strategies based on the internal and external

I

Show Your Leadership "Presence"

Stephen Denning

What is leadership presence? Is it something mysterious or magical? How did great actors and great leaders come to possess it? Were they born with it? Can it be learned?

Whatever it is, it's important. In their interesting book, *Leadership Presence,* Belle Linda Halpern and Kathy Lubar define presence as "the ability to connect authentically with the thoughts and feelings of others."

Make Good Use of Body Language

Be a "Dog Whisperer". If we're able to project our energy so that it energizes others, and so that our thinking, our feeling, our verbal messages, and our bodily movements are all congruent, that can hugely reinforce what we are trying to communicate. If our body language contradicts what we are saying, it will distract from or undermine our intended message.

One reason is that listeners are not just fluent readers of body language. They are acutely aware of the slightest bodily cues a speaker gives, wittingly or unwittingly, and can infer immediately what they mean. Remember when President George H. W. Bush glanced at his watch in the middle of a presidential debate in 1992? Viewers immediately jumped to the conclusion that Bush wanted the debate to be over. Whatever leaders communicate through their body language will usually speak louder than their spoken words, because listeners will conclude that the message conveyed through their body language is what the speaker really feels and means, even if they are saying something else.

Some of the more interesting insights on body language come from the world of animal trainers. Vicki Hearne's wonderful book, *Adam's Task,* notes that the people who come to visit the wild animals she works with fall into several categories. First, there are the people with super-sized egos, which she calls "Hollywood types": they are self-absorbed and indifferent to where they are. Their pompous strutting is essentially irrelevant to, and ignored by, the animals. Then there are the "researchers" who are testing abstract propositions on the animals. These people are, she says, "contaminated by epistemology." Around dogs, they are what she calls "bitees," that is, the people most likely to be bitten as a result of the dogs' frustration at their combination of intrusiveness and unresponsiveness. Finally, there are the "animal trainers," who exhibit soft, acute, 360-degree awareness of who they are and who else is there. In the very way they move, they offer mute acknowledgment of the presence of the animals and fit into the spaces shaped by their perceptions. It's precisely this "soft, acute, 360-degree awareness" that leaders need to exhibit in relation to the people they are seeking to lead.

What Hearne is talking about is the body language of leadership that Cesar Millan teaches to dog owners. What Millan is good at demonstrating in his amusing program, *The Dog Whisperer,* which can be watched on the National Geographic television channel or on the Web, is the calm assertiveness of leadership. In his program, owner after owner learns to establish "presence" through the calm assertive behavior that establishes someone as a leader.

Millan demonstrates with his own body language the difference between being assertive and being aggressive. The body language of aggressive behavior communicates the risk of some kind of imminent attack on the listener, as when the "look of an angry hawk" came over Howell Raines when he was talking to his staff. I don't believe Raines actually meant any harm, bodily or otherwise, to his listeners, but that's not what they took away from the encounter. If leaders' behavior looks aggressive, their listeners will wonder what's going to happen next. And they may be aggressive in response, perhaps not immediately.

The calm assertiveness of real leadership implies energy, but energy that has been harnessed, energy that offers no direct threat to the audience. Outward calm communicates an absence of hidden tensions with which the speaker is wrestling, hidden tensions that might break out at any moment and hurt someone. Calm assertiveness means confirming in our outward demeanor that we are in control of our own fears and desires. In acting thus, we show that we are there for the audience, ready to give them full attention, available to listen and to interact with them and to offer an invitation to the future. One piece of good news from Cesar Millan's work is that the agenda of things a leader has to learn is not huge. It's calm assertiveness, keeping your head held high, squaring your shoulders, maintaining appropriate eye contact, and being there for the dog. And what's even better news, once the dog owner does that limited number of things, the dog instantly accepts the dog owner as a leader.

The subtleties and nuances to learn about body language and presence are infinite and you could spend a lifetime steadily enhancing your mastery of them. But the immediate progress that can be made in taking care of the basics of the body language of leadership is enough for most leaders to move from "boring" to "extraordinary."

The most important element is eye contact. Leadership is a highly interactive phenomenon, and eye contact is the highway on which the interaction takes place. You look directly at the audience, person by person, without moving your gaze sideways, which may be interpreted as shiftiness. You establish eye contact with all the people in the room, particularly people in the back corners. You symbolize through eye contact that you are ready to converse with everyone who is there.

The second element follows from the first: Throw away your notes. You can't have eye contact with an audience if you are reading from notes. They are an obstacle to eye contact. They also symbolize a physical barrier between you and the audience. Any physical thing between you and the audience — even a piece of paper — blocks the flow of psychic energy. Moreover, if you are reading from notes, you can't be fully present. By reading from notes, you are signaling that you aren't speaking for yourself, from your heart; you are a messenger reading a message devised at another time. Perhaps the author was you — perhaps it was another person. It hardly matters; the overriding implication of reading from notes is that you are not fully present for the audience at this moment to interact with them. You have become a mere courier, not a leader.

Next, if you can, get out from behind any podium between you and the audience. Podiums get in the way of direct bodily communication. Like any physical object between you and the audience, they block the flow of psychic energy. Subliminally, the audience may see you as hiding from them. Let the audience see you without anything between you and them. Then make sure that you maintain an open body stance, square shoulders, relaxed, calm, assertive, with a total focus on the audience. By doing this, you signify that you are there for the audience. And if you are there for them, they will be there for you.

You use gestures to signify that it's not just your mind communicating. Gestures convey that your whole body is behind what you're saying. You make sure your gestures are in sync with the content of what you are saying. Gestures serve as a kind of visual punctuation to the words. They should also reflect contagious energy and enthusiasm. Stiff or jerky gestures may be interpreted as inner tension and lack of resolution. Here again, gestures should reflect calm assertiveness, signifying personal mastery of your message.

Finally, you plant your feet firmly on the ground and face the audience squarely and openly. If need be, wiggle your toes to remind yourself not to perambulate, which is massively distracting. In particular, don't walk from side to side across the speaker's platform. The audience will interpret this as restlessness, lack of calmness, and perhaps even a hidden wish to quit the room. If you must move, then move toward the audience to indicate a wish to be closer and more interactive with them. Choose different individuals in the audience and move toward them successively. This will be interpreted as a wish to connect and engage, rather than escape.

As leaders' skills mature, their experience becomes deeper and more meaningful, both to themselves and to their audience. They will not be able to say why precisely. But subtle, indefinable elements will enter into the performance, elements that weren't there before. They will succeed in putting more of themselves in what they say. They will find more resonance between themselves and their audiences. As performers, they will in a sense be getting better, even though leadership isn't really about getting "better."

Combining Graphics and Texts

Can Leaders Use Written Stories? Most of this book concerns oral communication. Can leaders use written communication to inspire enduring enthusiasm? It's not impossible, as Lincoln's Gettysburg Address demonstrates: a speech that was ineffective when delivered had profound and lasting effect in written form. And books have obviously had transformational effects over time. But in practice, in the hectic modern world where people want results now, reliance on the written word will generally be insufficient to inspire the kind of skeptical, cynical, or hostile audiences that one finds in today's workplace or marketplace to enduring enthusiasm for a cause. To engage these kinds of audiences with strange, new, transformational ideas, I have two words of advice: Be there!

PowerPoint is a powerful, infinitely flexible graphics program. The only practical limit on adapting it to any need is the imagination of the presenter.

This is not to deny that PowerPoint causes problems. In the 30 million or so PowerPoint slideshows that take place each day around the world, most are filled with illegible text, boring images and bland abstractions. It's these unsound practices that account for the dazed looks on the viewers' faces, not PowerPoint itself.

Should one forgo PowerPoint slides? It's true that the occasional speaker can mesmerize a crowd without any visual aids. The atmosphere can become like that of a circus tent. All eyes are on the presenter, who turns into a performer. The medium encourages the speaker to use theatrical tricks to keep the audience's attention. It can be an effective performance. But it is less likely that the message sticks as well as one that combines words with images. That's because some people simply respond better to images than words, while other people respond better to words than images. The evidence is not gender neutral; that is, the bell curves of men and women don't overlap. On average, women respond better to words than pictures. On average, men respond better to pictures than words. Obviously, there are exceptions — verbal men and picture-oriented women — but on average, that's what the data shows. As a result, if you want to reach the whole audience, it is a good idea to use both words and images.

"Charisma" is the Result of Leadership Rather than the Reason

Some writers wrongly consider charisma as an essential element of leadership. Charismatic leaders, it is said, appear "so extraordinary, due to their strategic insight, strong convictions, self-confidence, unconventional behavior and dynamic energy, that followers idolize them and want to become like them."

We have been living for a long time with the legend of the born leader, the colorful charismatic, the innate firebrand who walks into a room and electrifies everyone with their sheer physical presence. The fact is that the charismatics — such as Gandhi, Martin Luther King Jr., and Steve Jobs — lacked any particular physical characteristics that made them charismatic. Such people do exist in the world: the film star good looks of John F. Kennedy come to mind. But they are rare. The brute fact is that most successful leaders are quite ordinary in physical appearance. Overall, the idea that some kind of innate physical charisma is required for leadership is a pernicious myth.

Academic research confirms the same phenomenon at more mundane levels. For instance, Nancy Roberts of the University of Minnesota has written movingly of a highly successful school superintendent of a district in the Mid-West. When she was appointed to her position, the superintendent was not perceived as charismatic. It was only after she had been in the position for several years and the change process that she launched was well under way that people began to think of her as charismatic. This wasn't the inevitable result of extraordinary personal qualities but rather the result of her handling of the problems that the school district faced at the time.

Similar findings come from a five-year study by Warren Bennis and Burt Nanus of sixty top-level corporate leaders and thirty leaders of public sector organizations. Few of the individuals studied fitted the stereotype of a charismatic leader. They were not larger-than-life individuals. Most of them were very ordinary in appearance, personality, and general behavior. They were, however, strongly committed to a vision and reflected that commitment in their decisions and behavior.

Charisma is thus usually a consequence of leadership, not the cause of it. Once leaders have accomplished something, they appear to acquire qualities that no one noticed in them before. They seem to grow in size: people begin to look up to them and start talking about their charisma.

Gandhi was "a pilgrim on a quest for Truth, quiet, peaceful, determined, fearless, who would continue that quest and pilgrimage, regardless of the consequences." Gandhi "invested many of his gestures with special symbolic meaning, and at one point or another somebody has sanctified his every action and utterance, so that today in India — and elsewhere — there exists not one Gandhi, but hundreds of Gandhis."

Yet the extraordinary charismatic qualities that were so obvious in Gandhi after his achievements were apparently invisible to others before those achievements. He was a short, thin, and sickly child. He was an indifferent student who found schoolwork hard. He envied the big, strong boys who were good at sports like cricket and gymnastics, at which he performed poorly. A photo of him at the time shows not so much eyes that were pools of infinite sadness as eyes displaying a hunted, apprehensive look. With his large nose, he was an ugly young man, something that he eventually became proud of, claiming to be "the ugliest man in the world." He was married by his parents at the age of thirteen to a girl his own age, and, already demonstrating a healthy sexual appetite, consummated the marriage that night. He was a jealous and imperious young husband, forbidding his young wife to go anywhere, while declaring that he found her company tedious.

In England, Gandhi set out to become an Englishman. He bought Western clothes. He took up ballroom dancing. He took up elocution lessons for a while, but eventually concluded that his efforts to become an Englishman were futile. Instead he spent much of his time pursuing various vegetarian causes, "to the irritation of practically everyone, Indian or English, whom he came to know."

After three years in London, he returned to India, and he set up a legal practice, first in Rajkot and then in Bombay. When he finally obtained a case to argue, he stood in front of the court and couldn't think of a single question; he had to sit down and give the brief to a colleague. After that, he didn't get another case.

At this point in his life, Gandhi was the very antithesis of charisma. He was unattractive in appearance. He was graceless in manners. He was lacking in tact. In private, he was annoyingly persistent. In public, he was too shy to open his mouth. He was unable to earn an income as a lawyer. If his eyes were "pools of infinite sadness," there is no record of people noticing it at the time. The fact is that Gandhi's charisma was the result, not the cause, of his accomplishments. No one sensed an inkling of charisma until after he had made up his mind on what he wanted to do with his life, which occurred after an incident of racial discrimination in South Africa; he was holding a first-class ticket, but he was thrown off the train by a white guard at the request of a white man, and left shivering in a dark waiting room. Within a week of the incident, he convened a meeting of the Indians of Pretoria and delivered an address on white discrimination. It was his first public speech. Passion for the cause dissolved his shyness. He found the words needed to communicate his commitment. And so began his long journey as an agent of change, first in South Africa and then in India. It was only after he had success in influencing people that people began to think of Gandhi as having charisma.

About the Author

Stephen Denning, who enjoys the reputation of "The King of Telling Stories" in the Western business management community, is a strong advocate of "telling stories to enhance leadership". He is the author of the best-selling books *Squirrel. Inc*, *The Leader's Guide to Storytelling* and so on. His articles on "telling stories" were published many times in the *Harvard Business Review.* Stephen was chosen as one of the world's top ten most respected knowledge leaders and was listed as one of the world's 200 best management gurus, in the same league with Jack Welch, the CEO of General Electric. This article was originally published in the 12th issue of the *CEIBS Business Review* in 2009.

II

Mindfulness: The Quiet in the Eye of the Storm

Ben Bryant and Jeanny Wildi

The East and the West are converging not only materially — through global trade, virtual networks, manufacturing technologies and consumer fashions — but also psychologically — through development and integration of previously diverse views of the world. This convergence is nowhere as evident as in the work being done to integrate universal methodologies of leadership development.

At the center of the hurricane of economic globalization is the quiet space of mindfulness, a philosophy and practice which helps those exercising leadership to situate themselves calmly in the eye of the hurricane, where they are able to tap into the clarity and creativity that is necessary to ensure wisdom in decision-making and focused, authentic leadership.

What is "Mindfulness"?

> "On life's journey faith is nourishment, virtuous deeds are a shelter, wisdom is the light by day and right mindfulness is the protection by night." — Buddha

The notion of mindfulness has its origins within Buddhist traditions, where the technique has been developed for over 2,500 years as a powerful tool for self-development. The skill is acquired by being truly present in the here and now. As early as the 1940s, mindfulness entered mainstream Western psychotherapy with Gestalt Therapy. Today, Mindfulness Based Stress Reduction and Mindfulness Based Cognitive Therapy are only two of the many forms of mindfulness practices used in healthcare, management and organizational development. Studies have shown that "mindfulness" can bring significant changes to the brain, allowing people to have more flexible cognitive skills, be more creative and innovative, enjoy a higher level of well-being, have better abilities to control emotions, and be more tolerant and able to understand others.

"Mindfulness" can improve people's cognitive ability to deal with their emotions, strengthen their understanding of themselves and others, and improve their ability to analyze and solve problems. The application of "mindfulness" can help people to acquire the ability to "perceive (the) environment in a subtler way, and deal with the external world in a more flexible manner." The perception of the present through "mindfulness" can provide a richer and more viable environment, and transform people's habitual and subconscious behaviors into conscious behaviors.

The world is a complex place. This complexity appears to be increasing — and with it, our insecurity also increases. In the wake of these overwhelming demands, an organizational culture of fear emerges; we become anxious about our own competence and we become afraid of making mistakes and incurring the judgment of others. Since we feel overwhelmed by this rapidly evolving complexity of organizational life, our capacity to access mindfulness is overlooked.

In fact, the human mind is well-developed to "cope" with such complexity, although "simply coping" does not often lead to optimal effectiveness. If managers believe they do not have the time to work through all aspects of a problem, they are inclined to use cognitive shortcuts, which makes it easy to act on impulse, and causes them to rely more and more on familiar texts, diagrams, mental models, rules of thumb, habits and usual practices to help them adapt to the changes in their external environment.

Such cognitive mindlessness may feel like an inevitable response to a fast-paced, global world. Such "decisiveness" might even be mistaken for effective leadership, but it puts obstacles in the path of effective leadership by preventing awareness and adaptation to the multi-level reality before us. A corporate culture of cognitive shortcuts results in oversimplification, curtailed curiosity, reliance on engrained beliefs, and perceptual blind spots.

Relying on impulses is however not the same as relying on intuition. In taking cognitive shortcuts, managers' actions tend to become "mindless". For example, when you receive an email from an overseas colleague that annoys you, an impulsive response of sending an angry reply means that you are not able to understand your emotions and defensive capabilities at all. So acting on impulse makes it impossible for you to analyze the key issues of the problem, which, in this case, is to study what was going on with your colleague. This unconscious state can prevent managers from getting enough information and resources that could have been acquired, including signals from your own body. Being impulsive may make you feel better by temporarily removing the unpleasant emotions and thoughts. However, if you receive another response from that colleague at that moment, you will find yourself falling into a cycle of revenge and escalation.

The Core Elements of "Mindfulness"

In order to increase their effectiveness, leaders should become more mindful of what is going on in terms of their own thoughts, emotions and body, and what is going on in the context. These two approaches are based on the different traditions and practices of Western and Eastern philosophy and psychology. External mindfulness has its origins in the concrete Western orientation found today in cognitive and social psychology. Internal mindfulness has its origins in the ancient Eastern spiritual practice of meditation.

External mindfulness is being able to sense situations. It is being aware of the signals and cues in different contexts, noticing extraneous or unusual signs and paying attention to them. The self and the environment are continually treated as emerging and novel. Situation-sensing, along with subsequent reflection, helps us create a gap between our reactions and external reality.

Internal mindfulness is being aware of one's body, emotions and thoughts and requires the ability and attitude to monitor one's inner reality. Being aware of one's own mental responses to internal stimuli sounds easy, but in practice, it is not. The practice of mindfulness, whether external or internal, is based on a few key practices that are simple on the surface, but difficult to master.

Detaching from the Outside

The first step of mindfulness involves detaching from the outside world and from one's inner thoughts and emotions. There is a big difference between having a thought, or feeling an emotion, and being aware that you are having a thought, or being aware that you are feeling an emotion. An illustration of detachment could be that of watching a thriller movie. One can either be caught up in the web of emotions that the movie evokes, or one can step back and consider that this is a beam of light passing through a piece of moving celluloid which is projecting onto a screen with some sound and music that are designed to generate particular emotions. The latter would be an example of detaching yourself from the stimulus.

When we are caught up in our impulsive routines and the accompanying emotions in the midst of a complex situation, we tend to block out our receptiveness to internal and external data. We take a cognitive shortcut and become fixated on single external factors. We develop selective perception, and we are unable to see what is really going on.

Noticing

Once we have detached ourselves from the outside world and our emotions and thoughts, we develop the ability to notice things. Noticing is what young babies seem to do a lot of. Sometimes we see them fix their gaze on someone or something unfamiliar. The baby has no idea what to make of the stranger, and because of that, they are able to notice everything. We seem to lose the capability to notice without judgment as we grow older. We apply old formulas to new problems. Everything starts to look familiar — the same old thing — and when it is not familiar, we search for a familiar box to push it into.

"Noticing" means being able to take in impressions without immediately attaching meaning or adding judgment to them. This is very difficult for human beings. Our brains are constantly searching for meaning in everything we hear and see, so that we can simplify, evaluate, and decide what to do. Unfortunately, we all too often contaminate our own perceptions with unexamined assumptions we have already internalized. Noticing contributes to mindfulness by keeping us open to our experience of the external.

"Here and Now" Awareness

When faced with complex problems, we tend to multiply the sources and quantity of information available, and this frequently results in information overload. We become prisoners of too much cognitive input, when what we should do is improve the quality of the attention we give to the here and now. Psychologists have shown that people who are happier in life tend to be satisfied with what they have right now, rather than aspiring for something in the future and subsequently attaining it. "Here and now" awareness contributes to mindfulness by liberating mental energy and allowing us to pay heed to immediate experiences as they happen.

Mindfulness in Leadership Situations

During a meeting with the executive team, the CEO of a major utility company sensed high levels of power struggle and resistance in his team. After a prolonged debate, they had finally reached a consensus on the issue of a recent takeover — or so it appeared. Yet he noticed that the mounting dissonance had not truly subsided. He suspected that some emotional resistance remained under the surface, so he stopped speaking. He looked around the table into each team member's eyes and sat down. Then he said, "OK. Let's just drop this agenda today. What is really going on here, guys? How's everyone feeling right now?" At that point, the team members started to speak from their heart, describing what was going on for them. Everyone became more aware of what was happening within themselves and for each other. The conversation, which had been stuck until that point, became more exploratory and creative.

In this example, the CEO's mindfulness heightened his sensitivity to his own and his team members' emotional discomfort. Instead of automatically closing the meeting after it looked like they had achieved "consensus", he unexpectedly stopped the discussions with a surprising question that invited everybody into the present discussion. This leader responded by detaching himself and his team from the meeting agenda, noticing his surroundings and becoming aware of his present surroundings, and this allowed others to free themselves from the emotions and frustrations they had been holding. His meeting had technically ended, but he made the mindful choice to focus on detaching from what was apparently going on and focusing on what was really going on. The effect of this was liberating for everyone.

We are obsessed with control today — we are obsessed with controlling our careers, our employees, our finances, our future, our whole lives. We even try to control our spouses and children! But we have so little awareness of how our minds, emotions and bodies work to constrain our effectiveness as human beings and as leaders. Developing skills in mindfulness can take many years, as in the Buddhist traditions, but we stand to benefit immediately from discovering how to detach and develop a deeper sense of what is truly happening in the moment — both outside and inside us.

Mindfulness, as a skill, is a capacity within each of us that can be developed with practice. How does one develop this skill? The training involves disciplining ourselves to become more attuned to our immediate experience. It requires disciplining our minds to focus immediately and repeatedly on the awareness of thoughts, emotions and psychological processes through detachment, noticing our surroundings, and becoming increasingly aware of the here and now of our environment and of our bodily sensations, emotional feelings, and our thoughts and images.

Training methods — especially deeper behavioral methods employed at IMD in high-intensity leadership programs — that employ an awareness of mindfulness, facilitate the development of responsible leadership. As we begin to think and feel in a more nuanced and differentiated way, our behaviour becomes more spontaneous, tolerant, and flexible in engaging reality. Mindfulness allows us to exercise leadership more responsibly by letting go of habitual patterns and rapidly adapting our behavior to meet the demands of new and unexpected situations.

About the Author

Ben Bryant is Professor of Organizational Leadership at the International Institute for Management Development (IMD), Lausanne. **Jeanny Wildi** is an assistant researcher at the IMD. This article was originally published in the 10th issue of the *CEIBS Business Review* in 2009.

III

Stand Your Ground or Compromise?

Charles P. Garcia

Compromise is one of the few English words with contrasting meanings. According to Webster's Dictionary, "compromise" means "to find or follow a way between extremes", which sounds like a good thing. But the dictionary also gives another explanation, "to make a shameful or disreputable concession", something that cannot be considered good.

The choice of standing one's ground or making a compromise can be greatly difficult for leaders who cannot avoid it. Making a wrong choice in dealing with such critical issues can completely destroy leadership.

The Art of "Compromising to Settle a Difference"

As a White House scholar during the Reagan administration, Craig Coy (1983–1984 White House scholar) was assigned to work with Jack Svahn, the Presidential Domestic Policy Assistant, and Edwin Meese, the Presidential Adviser. Coy participated in almost all meetings of the Presidential Budget Review Committee; other participants included Chief of Staff James Baker, Edwin Meese, and David Stockman, Office of Management and Budget Director. The committee was working on a budget for the fiscal year 1985. Coy learned the most valuable leadership lessons during the process.

"I have learned why James Baker is able to get things done, and why his career has been so successful." Coy said, "There was a conflict about the drug enforcement budget for the Coast Guard. Meese was responsible for the drug enforcement policy committee. While he insisted that the Coast Guard needed US$100 million, David Stockman believed the budget was at most US$50 million. I was still working at the Coast Guard. They found me, and said, 'Let's talk to the president.' At the time I was in the Oval Office with President Reagan, James Baker, and Edwin Meese. When talking about how the Coast Guard needed the money, Edwin Meese turned to me and said, 'Craig, tell them why the Coast Guard needs funds.' I said that the Coast Guard was underfunded, with old ships and equipment. Our work efficiency could not improve without upgrading the equipment. But then Stockman tried to convince us that the Coast Guard's existing funds were enough. At this point, Baker said something crucial, 'Edwin, you know that it is pretty hard to get US$100 million right now, and David Stockman, you know that it is indispensable to have US$50 million. Then why don't we make a compromise to set the budget at US$75 million? By doing that, the president will be relieved, and you two will both be happy, right? The contradiction was solved just like that. James Baker showed me the art of compromise, a way to ensure everyone has got something, and to avoid an unnecessary decision for the president to make."

The Strength to Insist

What Coy learned at the White House is that compromising can prevent catastrophe and avert crisis. But Francis Harvey (1978–1979 White House scholar), another former White House scholar, learned the opposite: Sometimes the right choice is to refuse to compromise. Harvey was an engineer at Westinghouse Power before he was selected as a White House scholar. He was assigned to the Department of Defense to work with Minister Harold Brown. Brown was a smart but introverted scientist who served as the Defense Minister when President Lyndon Johnson was in power. "What I have learned from Dr. Brown is that you have to be well aware of your environment, because your understanding of things can't break away from your living environment, be it the market environment or the national security environment." Harvey said, "In the corporate world, there are many examples of leaders who make wrong decisions and place lots of stupid orders by being divorced from the market."

Harvey witnessed Brown's efforts to increase the defense budget despite President Carter's commitment to substantially reducing the budget after the Vietnam War. "In a considerably liberal and democratic governing environment at the time, the reason why Brown raised the defense budget was that he had already seen the intention of the Soviet Union." Harvey said, "I remembered all the fierce competitions about the balance of strategic nuclear weapons during the nuclear arms race. The Soviet Union would immediately chase after us once we were in the lead. We must maintain a long-term competitive advantage. The quantity did not matter, and what mattered was being on an equal footing. Minister Brown has done this, which made me admire deeply. It was evidence that he had been aware of the security environment."

After Harvey returned to Westinghouse Power at the end of the semester, he applied the experience he gained at the White House to his career. In the following 20 years, he played the roles of a great variety of executives at Westinghouse Power until November 2004 when he returned to the government service department and assumed the most important role of his life, Secretary of the United States Army appointed by President George Bush.

When Harvey was the Secretary of the United States Army, the Army's budget for 2005 was US$98.6 billion. Harvey was responsible for submitting a new five-year financial plan. Both the Office of Management and Budget and the Defense Minister tended to cut the Army budget. "From the beginning, my prior task was to improve the welfare of the soldiers and their families. As the Secretary of the Army, there were a lot of tough tasks waiting for me." Harvey said, "The Army was entering the Iraq War unprepared. As a leader, when you see the soldiers fighting in the battlefield, the one thought that occurs to you is that you have the obligation to provide the troops with the funds they needed. Sometimes you had to insist on your own opinion, which was something I did. I submitted the budget three and a half months later than scheduled, which gave me the reputation of disunity."

According to Peter Schoonmaker, Chief of Staff of the United States Army, "Competition often occurs among various government departments, but we can't lose. Instead of just saying that we were short of money, we showed the required readiness to them, and told them the specific cost to reach the readiness. These were visible and tangible issues. So when they tried to cut off the US$24 billion budget, we were able to show them the consequences for our armed forces in Afghanistan and Iraq. The guys who wanted to cut budgets were always trying to fight against the facts, but what we had was empirical data."

When the government's financial directives suggested that the Army cut its budget, Schoonmaker and Harvey were faced with three options: The first one was to reduce the members of the troops, the second one was to cut down establishment for army units, and the third one was to insist on their initial position to continue to ask for money. They chose the third option, refusing to submit the budget. Finally, their strategy succeeded. During Harvey's time as Secretary, the Army's budget more than tripled compared to what it had been 10 years ago, and the recruitment of army personnel became more effective.

Harvey launched a new recruitment plan with a fresh idea, which was turning the entire army into recruiters.

"In the business world, established employees are usually the best channel for recruiting new employees. Therefore, we started a program that rewarded each veteran who brought in a rookie with US$1,000. When our soldiers were on leave and returned home, they would tell their friends, 'Hey, the Army is really good. I am proud of my contributions to the country. I think you should also join us.' What a terrific idea! This method was really effective." In 2006, the active Army achieved unprecedented recruitment levels with 80,000 new soldiers. And the Army was approved to reach a permanent staffing of 547,000 soldiers in 2012.

President Reagan is another person who insists on the principle of not compromising under pressure. In 1981, nearly 13,000 air traffic controllers began a strike a few months after he took office. These people were federal employees who had complained about the management of the Federal Aviation Administration (FAA) for many years and demanded more generous welfare, higher salary, and fewer working hours. The government's position was simple; they did not plan to spend more money, nor did they plan to reduce working hours in exchange. When the negotiations between the trade union and the government came to a deadlock, the air traffic controllers ignored the law and started a strike, attempting to cause the paralysis of national air traffic.

Robert McFarlane (1971–1972 White House scholar) was a counselor for the State Department. He recalled that there were many different opinions on how to deal with the strike in the White House. President Reagan disagreed with the counselors' opinion. "Reagan said that the union's defiance of federal laws could not be tolerated. The air traffic controllers were irresponsible and put the country at risk. All of them must be dismissed. A majority of members of Cabinet advised him not to do this, which was politically stupid. Reagan replied that it was the right thing to do."

President Reagan completely ignored the concerns of the Cabinet members and held a press conference at the White House Rose Garden on the day of the strike. He issued an uncompromising statement to the air traffic controllers and delivered an ultimatum, "You are breaking the law. Return to work immediately within 48 hours or you will be dismissed." More than 11,000 strikers thought that President Reagan was bluffing, but he was not. Reagan fired them and permanently banned them from working at the FAA. Despite the union's public protest against the dismissal, most Americans supported Reagan's uncompromising approach to dealing with the law-breakers.

Compromising and Loyalty

Leaders need to learn when to stand one's ground and when to use the art of compromise. As former President Gerald Ford once said, "Compromise is the oil that makes governments go." White House scholar Nelson Diaz (1977–1978) learned how high-efficiency leaders conducted affairs flexibly from his mentor, Vice President Walter Mondale.

Diaz recalled that one day, he and Mondale had been flying to Los Angeles on Air Force Two to plan a birthday party for President Carter when they heard a surprising announcement: The President had just signed an arms sale agreement with Saudi Arabia. Mondale did not know Carter was going to consent to such a deal, and he knew it would be extremely unpopular with the Jewish community, of which Mondale was a strong supporter. "The Vice President had a choice to either turn the plane around or to continue on the trip," Diaz said. "Mondale consulted with Chief of Staff Hamilton Jordan, who was also on the plane, and we decided not to plan the birthday party but rather to proceed to Los Angeles to meet with Jewish leaders. When we got there the leaders were somewhat somber, but the Vice President explained President Carter's decision to them and asked how we could be more responsive to their concerns. He never gave a hint that he had no idea the deal was going to happen. He made something positive come out of it. I witnessed his loyalty to the President and his ability to compromise. Having been an activist on the streets I hadn't learned much about that, but on that trip I learned that sometimes half a loaf is better than no loaf at all," he said.

Diaz turned what he learned from the Vice President into action many years later when he held the post of the minister of Housing and Urban Development Department (HUD) and the general counsel of the White House scholar Henry Cisneros (1971–1972). As General Counsel to HUD, Diaz used litigation settlements to implement Cisneros' policies. Diaz arrived at HUD during the most litigious period in the department's history. He resolved 23 major cases that had been pending for a decade, and hired as his deputy the lawyer who had brought more suits against HUD than anyone else. "I wanted to demonstrate my willingness to be a listener and to develop a strong trust relationship so we could resolve all those cases," Diaz said. "And I was very aware that I had to use the art of compromise to resolve these very contentious cases. During my time at HUD I also applied what I learned from Vice President Mondale about the need to be loyal to your principal. Compromise and loyalty do go hand in hand. I learned that you must do everything you can to directly and openly engage the individuals with whom you disagree. However, loyalty demands that once a decision is made by the leader or a consensus is reached by the management team, you need to practice the art of compromise and proceed with the final decision as if it were your own."

Whether you're leading a business or a non-profit organization, a committee or a board, an athletic team or a family, you must learn when to compromise and when to stand firm. Although it's not possible to resolve every conflict through negotiation and concession, it is feasible in most cases. However, most things are not all or nothing, and there is no evident truth to tell you when and how to do the right thing, just as how the former Army Minister Harvey decided to insist on increasing the budget without making a compromise. In the end, everything is up to the leader's own judgment. As the proverb says, good judgment comes from experiences. Unfortunately, experience often comes from poor judgment.

The tougher decision is when not to compromise, which often puts your livelihood, your reputation, and the organization you lead at risk. While a leader must clearly stand firm on matters of integrity, if you can resolve the matter through give and take, while still staying loyal to your core beliefs, then find the middle ground. You'll soon discover what Judge Diaz already knows: Compromise is the art of making everyone a winner.

About the Author

Charles P. Garcia is a former White House scholar and author of the best-selling book *A Message from Garcia.* He was appointed by George W. Bush as a member of the Hispanic Education Excellence Committee. He is highly talented and has worked for prominent departments and heavyweights, including three presidential governments, cabinet ministers, governors, and a former North Atlantic Treaty Organization (NATO) Supreme Allied Commander. This article was originally published in the 9th issue of the *CEIBS Business Review* in 2009.

IV

To Be a Liberating Leader

Isaac Getz

Since kindergarten, people have been taught to resolve problems using top-down rules, listen to authoritative opinions and ignore their own thoughts, avoid self-expression beyond the minimum requirements as it can cause trouble; stay within the scope of duties as it is the safest path forward.... However, these are all old-fashioned ideas that need to be shattered by liberating leaders whose mission is to create freedom-form organizations.

Ewing Kauffman, founder of Marion Laboratories and the Kauffman Foundation, used to tell future entrepreneurs how, as a young sailor during World War II, he took the initiative to double-check his navigation officer's calculation of their location. In doing so, he broke an important safety rule and put his vessel at risk of being detected by a German submarine. However, through his actions, he saved three of his fleet's vessels from running aground. How should we balance the rules and freedom? This is the question raised by Kauffman.

The Story of FAVI

As a French copper alloy foundry with 600 employees, FAVI has acquired 80% of the global market share of transmission fork parts. Jean François Zobrist, former CEO of the company, tells the following story:

In 1985, in the initial stage of the cooperation between FAVI and F.I.A.T., the quality auditor of F.I.A.T. was going to pay a visit. According to the previous appointment, Zobrist would meet the auditor in Roissy Charles de Gaulle Airport. However, since the auditor had not contacted them, Zobrist returned home at 7pm.

When the auditor arrived at the airport at 8:30pm, he did not see anyone waiting for him. He called the company and a lady answered. He explained that his plane had been late, but the company had told him that someone would meet him at the airport. The lady who answered the phone confirmed the meeting place, picked him up at the airport and wished him good night after about an hour and a half.

"She is very friendly and polite. Obviously she doesn't pay attention to who I am or which company I come from," the auditor told Zobrist. After a few phone calls, Zobrist found out the "mysterious lady" was Christine, the janitor on duty that night. She had been cleaning the office in the factory when she received the call. Then she took the key to the company's car and drove to the airport. After sending the guest to the hotel, Christine returned to the company to complete the three-hour cleaning. She did not tell anyone about her egress.

Zobrist explained why Christine didn't tell anyone about her behavior: "This is quite normal for her. When the company faces a problem, she represents the whole company instead of only working as a janitor." Zobrist added that he did not thank her for doing this. "When you neither punish nor reward people's behavior, they will turn into daily behaviors that happen every day. Christine did not think that she had done something exceptional, and just went for it without thinking about asking for permission, or receiving acknowledgment."

At FAVI, employees enjoy complete freedom and responsibility to solve problems. Over the years, similar behaviors have greatly benefited FAVI, in the areas of outstanding product quality, on-time delivery and considerable growth. A significant share of the company's revenue is shared with employees in the form of an annual bonus which is usually equivalent to 4-month or 5-month salary of employees.

We have visited a series of organizations like FAVI that have managed to maintain employee initiative, and refer to them as "freedom-form organizations." The leader of a free organization is given the name of "liberating leader."

Wisdom to Resolve Contradictions

Successful liberating leaders have three important characteristics: free and responsible values, creativity and wisdom. Since the first two characteristics are shared by many successful leaders, we will not discuss them in details. The key issue that will be analyzed is "wisdom", a quality which is uncommon in the research of leadership.

The key to wisdom is to hold contradictions. Wisdom is different from intelligence (the ability to acquire or process information). A person can be smart and foolish at the same time. Wisdom researchers define it as "excellent judgments, advice, and comments that integrate personal and public interests with difficult and uncertain life and behavior." Wisdom is helpful in solving uncertain, conflicting and contradictory goals, which requires a holistic and dialectical way of thinking.

Following the school of Aristotle, Western education has developed the notion that a proposition and its opposition cannot logically be true at the same time. However, East Asians do not fully agree with such logic. According to Lao Tzu, the founder of Taoism, "The greatest power seems weak/The purest white seems tainted/The abundant seems empty/The stable seems shaky/The certain seems false." Developmental psychologists have shown that the biggest problem for policymakers is to think about a problem in both a holistic and a dialectic way. That is, to consider the problem in relation to the surrounding environment (holistic thinking), while at the same time boldly thinking about it from two apparently contradictory perspectives (dialectical thinking) to help them move forward. Understanding these two dimensions of wisdom can help us learn how the concept of contradiction benefits the liberating leader.

In addition, the liberating leadership explains another contradiction: the coexistence of soft and hard ways of acting. For example, the liberating leader such as Zobrist has completely changed the management practices of enterprises with non-threatening and gradual methods. At the same time, Zobrist is able to behave quite decisively and openly when taking drastic measures to deal with certain dictatorships.

Liberating Leadership Quartet

Successful liberating leaders use wisdom to resolve a variety of conflicts. But the purpose for leaders to utilize wisdom is not only reform, but also the establishment of a free organization to perfectly combine the company's common interests and employee's personal interests. How should liberating leaders build and maintain freedom-form organizations?

Create an Equal Internal Environment. Jeff Westphal, CEO of Vertex (a global leader in tax software and services), who has created an internally equal business environment, talks about how he started the "liberated movement".

In 1993, when Westphal began to operate Vertex, the core software development project was a complete failure. While preparing to use his power to "tell" the team that they had "to redouble their efforts, step back, re-organize, and ... go right back at it," Westphal remembered something Stephen Covey had written in *Seven Habits of Highly Effective People*. He attempted to set aside all judgement, to imagine himself in others' places and to listen to them, and suddenly had an epiphany: "I realized in that instant that I never really understood anybody. I understood what I wanted to understand about them, rather than who they really were and what their needs were.... The application to business was instant: 'I'm walking around thinking I get it. But I don't get it. And other people are walking around thinking they get it, but they don't get it.'" So, instead of "tell, tell, tell," Westphal decided to try something different: "I came to work the next day ... and I started listening.... The very first 'program' that we implemented was that I changed my behavior. I started listening, I started actually involving people in my decision making, me personally."

The most fundamental advantage is that when people are genuinely listened to, they feel that they are being treated as intrinsically equal. They feel that their experience, knowledge, and ideas are as valuable as those of the head of the company.

The next step is to turn the manager who gives orders into a listener, which is more difficult for liberating leaders. Formal or informal training can be used to achieve this goal. Gore & Associates is a leading company in polymer production. Its founder and CEO, Bill Gore, introduced a regular dinner system to train managers to learn to listen to others with

Socratic questions. However, while liberating leaders continue to guide the transformation with wisdom, some managers are still using the authoritative "command-control" approach to management. In order to deal with these managers, Zobrist from FAVI and Robert McDermott from United Services Automobile Association (USAA), the fourth-largest auto insurer, chose to transfer them into job positions without subordinates on the condition that they keep their original salary.

Liberating leaders also need to eliminate certain routines that do not meet the equal needs of employees, such as fixed seating arrangements, senior offices for senior executives and managers, reserved parking spaces, hierarchical organization charts, and titles. Some management practices can also be removed, such as human resources management and its management procedures, travel expense application and expense list reporting, budgeting process, finance department and long-term planning process. Of course, these issues cannot be removed in only one step. In the early founding stage of Finland's second-place cleaning company, SOL, the company's budget was still a combination of uncontested individual manager budgets. It wasn't until 2008 that SOL announced that it had given up on the full budget, and that managers only needed to provide sales and profit forecasts. The company gave them complete freedom to decide the best way to achieve the desired goals.

The first guiding principle used by liberating leaders in the process of designing company is fundamental equality so as to turn employees into self-motivated individuals who can take free actions. But it also raises a new question: How to ensure that the employees take actions to maximize the benefits of the company?

Share the Company's Vision. To make good daily decisions, employees must understand what is best for the company's interests. Without such information, they may make decisions based on their limited personal experience. For example, certain decisions will be made just for the purpose of saving money for the company. While such decisions certainly apply to companies like Southwest Airlines, it is not suitable for businesses like Gore & Associates whose strategy is to lead an industry through excellent products and good customer relationships. Therefore, liberating leaders must attach great importance to explaining and sharing the company's vision to each and every employee.

We find that all companies with liberating leadership have a world-class vision. For example, Bob Davids, founder and chairman of Sea Smoke Cellars, a winery that has ranked among the top 100 global brewing companies for four consecutive years, said, "I am willing to spend the time and money needed to guarantee quality to put our company at the top of the market."

It is easy to explain a world-class vision, but much more difficult to share it with employees and make them truly accept it. Liberating leaders start to share their visions in the process of recruiting employees. When welcoming the new staff on the first day, Jeff Westphal from Vertex will tell them, "Welcome to Vertex. You are free to leave." What he wants to convey is that when employees find a more compelling career vision, they should no longer stay in Vertex. Vertex often provides assistance to employees who wish to pursue other goals, such as starting a business on their own.

Liberating leaders must follow their words with reinforced actions. Kris Curran from wine manufacturer Sea Smoke Cellars once put Bob Davids' vision to the test. She said to the CEO, "Yes, Bob, we have heard numerous times about your vision. But you would rather spend more than US$20,000 to beautify the landscape than allow me to spend an extra US$200 buying a wine hose." Hearing Curran's words, Davis asked her to prepare a list of the first-class brewing equipment she needed. Curran made "a just outrageous list of things". Davids browsed through the listed items one by one and discussed each new fixture, pump and bucket for 6 hours, and then asked Curran, "Well, when will you start to buy these materials?"

Curran, still skeptical, said, "So you won't stop me?"

Davis once again repeated his philosophy of freedom: "No, I believe your reason that new equipment can produce better wine. I will give you everything you need so you will not come back to me and use this as an excuse, 'If you allowed me to do that, things would be better.'"

Curran recalled, "I was suddenly baffled because I have never seen any employer who can truly abide by their promises in the past 8 years of working in this industry."

It is also necessary to develop leaders who deliver and enhance vision throughout the organization so as to reinforce the vision. As an early employee of Gore & Associates, Les Lewis was one of those responsible for delivering the company's vision. In the beginning, he learned the importance of on-time delivery from CEO Bill Gore. Gore is known for his extremely quiet manners, but when someone proposed that "it (was) okay to reach the 85% on-time delivery rate (instead of the full rate of delivery)," he raised his voice and refuted him. Gore's approach affected Lewis. So when Lewis found out that some new employees held the view that a 100% on-time delivery rate would mean having to go over the budget, he reminded these newcomers that on-time delivery was not an economic decision, but one of the company's core principles. Lewis's efforts ensured that Bill Gore's vision was accepted by other colleagues.

Finally, in order to maximize the emotional acceptance of the vision, liberating leaders need to be very generous in sharing relevant information. Richie Deerinck, the former CEO of Harley Davidson, regularly visits the American factory where he holds meetings to provide information and answer questions for each shift worker. The current CEO Jim Ziemer also follows this practice.

Sharing the company vision helps employees determine what kind of behavior would best benefit the company, which in turn allows them to take free actions responsibly. But then comes the next question: are they capable of doing this?

Create an Environment that Can Meet Employees' Growth Needs. In 1960, McGregor compared the impact of traditional "industrial production methods" and "agricultural production methods" on human development. According to him, "The individual will grow into what he is capable of becoming, provided we can create the proper conditions for that growth." Liberating leaders need to work hard to build an environment for growth of people's capabilities.

In 1967, McDermott became the CEO of USAA, a then under-performing auto insurer. He was firmly convinced that all of the company's services needed to be delivered in the first line, and the top-down model would not bring good results. McDermott began to rebuild the hierarchy by removing authoritarian managers, eliminating unfair and distrustful controls, equalizing the salary for male and female employees, and implementing a 40-hour work week to allow mothers to spend more time with their children.... These new systems met employees' needs for fairness, which in turn prompted them to accept the vision of "USAA is committed to being a world-class company."

However, most employees lacked the skills and knowledge to answer both insurance and financial questions as well as the practical operational problems that customers raised over the phone. In order to meet employees' needs for growth, McDermott introduced training and educational activities. As a strong believer that "everyone has a talent for something," McDermott firstly encouraged people to enter the field that attracted them, and then accept training according to their needs. He worked with local universities to provide employees with work-related courses (paid for by the company). In particular, service representatives were required to accept up to 16 weeks of training and simulation activities before they began to answer calls, including one week of on-the-spot telephone calls.

Treated equally, USAA's employees are accustomed to "to serve others as you'd like to be served," in accordance with the company's guidelines. The environment created by McDermott promotes employee growth and enables employees to provide the best service they can.

Employees might have the willingness and capability to engage in the best course of actions in accordance with the company's interest, but a problem may hinder this, which is the lack of authority to empower their act. This requires the company to give employees self-directing power.

Create an Environment that Can Meet Employees' Needs to Self-direct. If employees' work environment does not give them space for self-direction, they will not be self-motivated, nor will they act in accordance with the company's best interests. For example, at USAA, creating an environment conducive to self-directed behaviour included giving customer service staff the right to decide how long it takes to resolve a customer's problem. Therefore, unlike most call centers where the performance of customer service staff is evaluated by the number of calls processed per hour, the USAA assesses performance based on the number of issues the staff solve when the customer first calls. Staff can pay the claim even if the customer does not have any formal proof, and they also have the right to cancel an insurance policy that the customer does not realize is unaffordable at the time of signing. Such an environment is designed to meet employees' needs for self-direction and allows employees to motivate themselves to act in the interests of their customers and the company.

Other liberating leaders have different criteria for meeting employees' needs for independence. Bill Gore encouraged them to act independently by asking employees "whether they had made any mistakes recently." If the answer was "no", he would say, "You have not taken enough risks." When Bob Davids said, "I am going to go out for 8 months... If you feel like you have very important things to contact me to participate in your issue, what I want you to do is to have a rest. When this feeling disappears, I hope that you stand up, solve the problem, and then send me a solution by email," he was also encouraging self-direction.

It is a key issue for liberating leaders to meet the needs of employees for self-direction in order to successfully build a freedom-form organization. Failing to apply this guideline often leads to the failure of freedom-form organizations. One of the important reasons leading to the failure is that the leader did not make enough effort to support the culture he established.

To be a Cultural Manager. It is a long-term process for liberating leaders to start from building a freedom-form organizational environment to make most employees self-motivated and prompt them to act in the best interests of the company. Our research shows that it takes at least one year to achieve this, and 3 to 10 years to make it an indispensable identification. The liberating leader still plays his role even if a freedom-form organizational culture is established. For example, Bob Davids refused to make final decisions from the start so as to create an environment in which employees make their own decisions. When he saw that all employees were acting freely in the best interests of the company, he shifted his role, saying, "My job now is the keeper of the culture. I do it by talking to everybody every day: 'Hello, how are you, how's it going, what do you need?'" David Kelley, founder and chairman of the industrial design company IDEO, said: "My job is to maintain culture, which is the most important thing... Other things are distractions."

Liberating leaders don't think that people can change the views they learn in kindergarten in a few years, such as resolving problems through top-down policies and rules instead of the initiative of individuals or groups. Liberating leaders should be vigilant to those who were educated in the traditional education system at all times so that policies and rules do not slip back to the original.

Gordon, the former CEO of Chaparral Steel, a Texas mini factory, once "managed for 3%." He explained that the experience of catching a secretary who brought office supplies to her son as study materials made him issue a regulation: A ban on ordering office supplies in the summer. He estimated that the secretary would not have any office supplies to take away when the new semester began in September. Unfortunately, this rule also punished those who did not make mistakes. Also, the new regulation undermined the atmosphere in which employees were treated equally, trusted, and cared for, putting free organizations at risk. The liberating leader refused to "manage for 3%." Instead, they fired the wrongdoers.

The liberating leaders built a free environment by launching a quartet of organizational liberation. Harriet Quarty, founder and former CEO of Quad Graphics, a leading commercial printing company in North America, once said, "It is a company that relies on employees and for employees, not a company operated by the management." In such an environment, the consideration of private interests and the interests of others is integrated into the behavior of employees, making the company operate well.

About the Author

Isaac Getz is a professor at ESCP European Business School. This article was originally published in the 9th issue of the *CEIBS Business Review* in 2010.

V

Leaders Who Do Not Have Decent Work

Simon Caulkin

What role should the CEO play in promoting management borders and organizational design in a highly innovative organization? Simon Caulkin reveals the answer to us through the study of three rebellious leaders who take the unusual path.

Tim Brown and IDEO: The Most Innovative Business

IDEO, headquartered in California, USA, is considered a company with boring managers and poor management, but this has not prevented the company from becoming one of the world's largest and most innovative companies. According to a recent statistic, more than 550 designers from IDEO were nominated for Industrial Design Excellence Awards by *Business Week*. The number of nominations is more than twice as that of its main competitors. IDEO often ranks high in the list of "most innovative companies" according to media.

There is no doubt that the leaders of IDEO are aware of the reasons for their business success, which is the thin-type company management style. When asked about IDEO's secret, its founder David Kelley said,

"I just hired some smart people and then exited." He expressed the desire to establish a company where he could work with friends.

So, if not "management", what has bound the company together? One word, culture. According to Tim Brown, current CEO of IDEO, "the success of our business entirely depends on the company's culture." What kind of culture is it? Brown said, first of all, just like the other rebellious leaders around him, that he is neither a trained manager, nor a talent who dreams of being a manager. He studied art and had a dream to be a painter. He said, "management is just a tool to assist people to do what they want."

"T-shape" Dominates. As a design company, IDEO takes projects as its basic work, similar to consulting companies like McKinsey. But IDEO has many unique features. First of all, "the key to our culture is maintaining a long-lasting interest in new work," and keeping a repulsive attitude to bog-standard work, no matter how much money can be earned from that project. Brown admitted that this could be a challenge for IDEO, who needed to grow and learn, but the company's performance was good on the whole.

The second key point, according to Brown, is "making people with completely different backgrounds highly collaborative," something they seem to have discovered by accident. One factor to guarantee this is a detailed selection process. IDEO tends to recruit those "T-shape" talents who not only have preeminent skills, but take great interest in the environment they are in. "I-type" talents do not suit IDEO. In the rare event that an "I-type" talent entered the company, they would eventually leave due to an inability to adapt to the tense, experimental, and highly collaborative small-team work mode. No one is fully controlled in such an environment, and everyone contributes to the company from a specific aspect of design.

As for the third cultural characteristic of IDEO, its innovative model is borne out of emergency rather than planning. "In our company, no one will say which new field we are entering into today, as our ideas are just coming from brainstorms. At a partner's meeting, we tried to outline all the things that were going on in our companies; not those things that customers pay us to do, but what we truly have interest in. In fact, all of these projects go beyond the constraints of time and space for us. At some level, it seems like a mess, but we also see the incredible values brought by the approach of emergency innovation."

Forgiveness. The foundation which supports IDEO's unique innovative culture is the confluence of deep trust that is embedded in the company's DNA. This deep trust is partly the result of Kelley's original intention to work with friends. It also comes from his deliberate efforts to create an organization that actively encourages employees to embrace innovative adventures, even if it comes in the form of a task from annoying customers, which is not advocated in other places. "David often teaches us to apologise rather than seek permission." Brown said, "Go ahead and do things. If things get bad, apologize when necessary. But it is entirely up to you to evaluate whether a thing is good or bad, whether you want to do it or not at the beginning."

Can such a culture spread? If yes, how far can it spread? For example, organizational culture is receiving constant attention in Google. On the one hand, Brown admits that from the perspective of pure efficiency, IDEO does not have great performance. The experimental spirit means a lot of confusion, and the digestion of emergency experiences also requires a large amount of time and business travel. At present, this has not affected the company's growth, because IDEO finds that many of its cooperating partners are large and strong companies that share similar interesting problems. At the same time, Brown claims that some progress has been made in the development of the knowledge system to manage and utilize the company's accumulated experience.

Next station, the world. However, there is an immediate problem. According to Brown, the vast majority of new employees are not really interested in solving the innovation problems in big companies. The innovative issues they desire to solve include African agriculture, India's clean water and health issues, and education in North America. "So we now have an urgent need to adjust our business model to cater to the interests of our employees. Today 85% of our business comes from large Western companies. If we still need to maintain the proportion after 5 years, the company will reduce the scale in half; otherwise we can't retain employees of our current quality. So the challenge for us is how to integrate business models with our employees' passion. Because it is our original strength to develop the company."

Interestingly, Brown believes that IDEO's endless innovative thoughts need to break new boundaries in innovation, and the results will be critical. Regarding the real issue of scale, he said, "It's not about sharing information, but sharing inspiration. We are more likely to grow and develop if we can find a mechanism to share inspiration. I am very satisfied with our discoveries at this stage."

Vineet Nayar and HCL Technology Company: Explosive Growth

If you're a 2-billion-dollar service-oriented company struggling for the ever-increasing customer demand, how should you deal with the situation when your supplier's technology is becoming more and more complex, while at the same time you are losing one-quarter of the employees every year due to the fast-growing business? You should "destroy the CEO's office" and tell your customers that your employees come first.

Vineet Nayar, the CEO of HCL, an Indian IT and software development technology company, proposed the above view on Halfmoon Bay Forum.

HCL began to wake up in 2005, under the background of India's software market growing by 25% per year (and the export value was about US$40 billion). In a company with 35,000 employees, 8,000 employees will leave each year in order to maintain the annual business growth of 40%. The complexity of technology has hugely increased just like the market demand. According to Nayar, recent data shows that an aggregator needs to be familiar with 862 technologies to be customer-centered — "Google, Hewlett-Packard and Microsoft have produced complicated and incompatible products that give you more problems from time to time."

Combat commercialization. HCL had unexpected discoveries in the face of complexity. The company realized that IT service had become a commercial, high-tech market, but there was no real differentiation among suppliers. All the suppliers said they wanted to be customer-centered, "but in addition to talking about this, what other innovations can you make from the perspective of service?"

According to the result of Nayar's consideration, they might be completely wrong. There is no need to adjust to customer needs or other new problems. "Those who can truly give us a solution are our employees.

The most valuable thing for the whole industry is to deal with the situation when employees meet customers. The interactive interface between them is where the value is created. Employees with higher quality, better ability, greater efficiency and more active participation can create more value."

Men in The Mirror. As Nayar said, the first step to reverse these things is to learn from fairy tales. "We have spent a lot of time talking nonsense and telling everyone how great our company is. We launched a grand concept called 'Mirror, Mirror' to reveal many problems hidden in the company to all the staff. I have witnessed all of these things. This process has helped us release unprecedented energies, but it is really necessary to be honest. Therefore, 'Mirror, Mirror' is a question we often need to ask, which keeps us honest."

This logic points to the full democracy of the organization, a view that many companies are afraid of. Unlike Gore or Whole Foods Market, which has been operating for nearly 30 years with a traditional hierarchy system, HCL proposes a solution of making deep cultural reforms through a series of innovations instead of comprehensively adjusting the operational structure of the company.

Reverse Accountability System. To prove that they are serious about putting employees first, the company has launched a 360-degree assessment for all the managers before publishing the results online. In the past three years, approximately 20,000 employees have participated in the survey to grade 1,500 managers including Nayar in terms of 20 employee-related performances. Though the survey is not linked with salary or promotion, each manager has to take it seriously as it is made public. Based on the survey results, they try to overcome their shortcomings, or change direction in certain things, such as transforming into a technology-oriented leadership.

Committed to various kinds of accountability, Nayar has an internal blog, "Nayar Q&A", that allows employees to ask questions about anything in the company, and all conversations are posted on the company's internal network. The key issue is that all questions and answers will not be attacked.

Corporate Levels Parallel. Nayar said, "We are suspicious of what corporate hierarchy can surely bring us. Desiring to break out of the situation where one person has the final say, we started a plan called 'To Destroy the CEO's Office.' We created a levels-parallel organization that included 32 interest groups in which people could collaborate with each other and create opportunities outside the hierarchy system. In this way, decisions cannot be controlled by one person. Today, after three years, 20% of HCL's revenue comes from ideas and initiatives produced by interest groups."

Signing the Agreement. Everyone can easily say that employees come first, but they may also hear doubts like how to prove they put employees first. HCL's answer is a novel one, which is signing service level agreements (SLAs) between the executives and employees. For any complaint or consultation, employees can issue a service notice through the company's website to the department that needs to respond. Importantly, only employees have the right to shut down the notification. Since the department's service quality entirely depends on the response rate and speed of service notice, this method encourages various departments to respond as quickly as possible to shut down the notification. According to Nayar, by lessening the company's bureaucracy through SLAs, the company sends signals to support the front-line employees who create value for the company. Employees have played an increasingly active role in encouraging departments to be more forward-looking. In the long run, organizations will truly be employee-centered.

Jeffrey Hollender and Seventh Generation: Inspiration and Reflection

The Seventh Generation Company does not allow itself to live an easy life. Its products are daily necessities, such as toilet paper, disposable diapers and laundry detergent. But the company claims to produce sustainable products with multiple added values. As such, its products are not sold at Walmart. The company's operations are so transparent that its attorneys have to be particularly careful every time they speak publicly.

Jeffrey Hollender, President and Chief Creative Officer of Seventh Generation, said the company's name was taken from the "Iroquois Code", meaning that people should consider the impacts of their decision on the next seven generations no matter what they do. "During the past

10 years," he said, "all the advertising agencies have advised us to give up this name. Thank god we did not."

Basic Paradoxes. A paradox facing Seventh Generation is that the more it goes against the traditional business model, the better it operates. Following its founding 20 years ago, the private company has experienced losses for consecutive 12 years. As a private company, Seventh Generation does not disclose its finances. However, in the late 1990s, the company grew at a rate of 25% per year, and the number reached 45% last year. The rate may be even higher this year. How can it grow with this paradox?

According to Hollender, the reason is transparency. One of the three elements that represent the "essence" of the Seventh Generation is authenticity, which gives rise to the need for extreme transparency that drives everything (the other two elements are justice and fairness). Transparency means to not cover up something bad but to make sure that everyone knows it. But this is not enough. For example, if the company is trying to remove a chemical element from laundry detergent, the stakeholders must be invited to participate in the conversation. "Transparency motivates us to check everything we do and put all the issues people might be concerned about or ignore on our website," said Hollender. "The idea of being so self-critical and transparent is completely counter-intuitive. But I think people in our world are skeptical and distrustful, and transparency can produce the opposite effect by creating a certain level of trust and comfort, a relationship rarely established between consumers and product manufacturers."

Reflection and Focus. All of these are not easy. Hollender admits that not everyone can accept the culture of extreme self-reflection and telling the truth featured at Seventh Generation. "I told my analysts that as long as we are still on this road, I will never give up. The reason is that in Seventh Generation where criticism and self-reflection are always in place, it is easy for senior managers to return to the ready-made business model they have acquired from other companies. I often joke that the people we are hiring are being destroyed by their former company." He said, "When you hire a person and you tell him that you want them to be honest and straightforward, they will not believe you; they will say 'yes, I have heard this before, and I will never be fooled again.' It takes a few years to win trust from others."

But they will have unlimited benefits if they can do this. People are not only passionate about their work, but are excited about the fact that the company encourages them to do what they want — "This is one of the things I am proudest of and happiest about." "To be what you want to be" is also what Seventh Generation tries to tell its customers. Hollender acknowledged that continuous self-analysis can focus the company's thoughts. The company has worked very hard to understand the purchasing decisions customers make, which is different from traditional customer concerns. "We believe that establishing a great relationship with our customers is building a process in which they can become who they want to be and live the lives they want. Few companies can really understand customers with such ambitions. But there is indeed a huge opportunity in this regard, especially in the industry like ours."

Comment: Attempt to "Ignore Proper Occupation and Run Irrelevant Business" — Zhi Weiyong

There is no doubt that this proposition will be jeered at when it is first proposed. Based on the mindset of the Chinese, people are expected to "exert themselves in their work" and "strictly observe their duties." Otherwise they would be "get paid for doing nothing" and "fail to live up to people's expectations."

But sometimes it is hard to define what a "proper occupation and relevant business" looks like. 20 years ago, the best students in China chose to major in electrical automation; 10 years ago, the first choice of the top students in high school was often life science; today, economics and management are the most sought-after majors. So the "proper occupation" chosen by teenagers who are just beginning to plan their life course has undergone several rounds of change in accordance with societal trends, which can be explained by the lyrics of Faye Wong: "Nothing lasts forever."

Literatis in the Wei and Jin Dynasties either floated and sank in the official seas to pursue their bureaucrat career, or returned to the pastures to live with plum trees and cranes. Both of them are regarded to have held proper occupations, because they have similar pursuit of and concerns about their country and people, either inside or outside the imperial court.

It seemed that the only relevant business was "*to worry about the country's fate ahead of other people, and enjoy the pleasure after the people take delight in national prosperity.*" However, Xu Xiake, a person who had crossed the mountains and waters alone for several decades without aiming to earn an official title or literary fame, eventually completed the immortal work, *The Travel Diaries of Hsu Hsia-k'o*. Another example is Xu Guangqi, who not only worked as an official, but also translated *Elements* into Chinese, compiled the *Agricultural Policy Book,* and introduced sweet potatoes to Central China in his spare time. These were considered as improper occupations at the time, but hundreds of years later, when the tottering Qing government began to realize that the most urgent "proper occupation" was natural science, Xu Guangqi became the pioneer of the movement of "Spreading Western education to the East".

Whether the work is proper or improper should not be constrained by the public's expectation. As Xu Guangqi said, "The scholar-bureaucrats of Confucianism are looking down on practical business."

Returning to the topic of management, the three CEOs mentioned in this article may be considered to have "ignored proper occupations and ran irrelevant businesses" because they have spent too much energy in organizational design and corporate culture. In fact, this is more like a view held by Chinese. Chinese entrepreneurs always regard innovation, leadership, and organizational reform as "irrelevant business". As Xie Zuyu from Boss Booz & Company concludes, "What Chinese companies have focused on during the past three decades were indicators of hard power, such as scale, output, low cost, financial strength, functional brand and technological superiority, but they failed to put in enough effort in developing soft power, such as the development of leadership and innovative management style, and the construction of a technology ecosystem."

With such a preconceived attitude, many things have actually become more and more improper and irrelevant. Most of the management tools such as Six Sigma and Balanced Scorecard came to a hasty and disastrous end in Chinese enterprises. A majority of reports by the consulting were carefully crafted only to support the decision makers' decisions.

Of course, there is no need to be overly pessimistic. The best companies in China have begun to learn to "run irrelevant businesses."

"Making a profit" is supposed to be the "most proper and relevant business" for companies, but Ma Yun recently set a "revenue ceiling indicator" for Taobao and Alipay. The executives' salary is not allowed to rise beyond a certain level, otherwise they will be punished. This policy is aimed at restraining the excessive income growth of the two companies, since Ma Yun believes it is not the right time to pursue profits, because the cake will continue to grow bigger when the company put money into the market. In addition, Alibaba is now concerned about whether its corporate culture can be effectively passed down. According to a vice president of Alibaba Group, currently their biggest concern is the weakened corporate culture due to the rapid expansion of their business scale, since "it is hard to make 500 established employees affect 2,000 newcomers." Therefore, Alibaba is enthusiastic about holding meetings to discuss theories and talk about business strategy and culture. It is said that many people are so emotionally involved in the meetings that they even "cry and shed bitter tears."

About the Author

Simon Caulkin is editor of *The Observer*. This article was originally published in the 6th issue of *CEIBS Business Review* in 2009.

VI

Reformers that Step Down from the Altar

Liu Xue

The impression people have of reformers is often derived from their noble, just and unquestioned motives. Therefore, attention is mostly focused on the control of the reform process, and the sources of resistance to reform. But little attention is paid to the leaders of reform (or reformers) themselves, such as their motives, resources, and capabilities, all of which are factors that can influence the destiny of reform.

In fact, this assumption fails to see the whole picture that is overshadowed by the trivial, preventing people from discovering the root factors leading to the success or failure of some reforms. Such views may result in poor reform movements being initiated by the wrong people at the wrong time in the wrong place.

We hold the view that reformers' understanding of their motives is significant only in rationalizing their own behaviors; rather, it is the members' perception of a reformer's motives that can truly determine their attitude and willingness to participate in the process of reform. With a given motive, the power to lead organizational members depends on the reformer's individual capability and resources he owned.

Not all top managers are qualified to launch major reform. Their position will be changed if they fail to change their minds. Nor is every reformer able to easily give an impassioned speech. To achieve the final success of reform, reformers need to have motives that truly represent the core objectives of the organization and reflect the underlying needs of the majority of its members. Managers should be able to formulate appropriate strategies based on the internal and external environment organizations face, as well as the capabilities and resources of the individual to effectively control the reform process.

Power, the Foundation of Reform

The so-called strategic reform refers to the process in which the basic factors to realize the goal have experienced adjustment and change, such as organizational structure, resource allocation, action system, and organizational culture. Here we specifically use a neutral definition of reform, change. Change is not necessarily good, such as the disastrous damages caused by civil war within the enterprise; similarly, opposition to change is not always a bad thing, such as resistance to improper goals and strategies of reform. Whether it is good or bad depends on the motives, goals, strategies, and outcomes of the strategic reform. Has it improved the organization's ability to adapt to the external environment, strengthened its ability to sustain development, and enhanced organizational performance? Or it is the other way around?

The reason why we put emphasis on the neutral nature of reform is that it has been inappropriately glorified and sanctified. It is being taken for granted that reform occurs because of justice, morality, and greatness. Meanwhile, reformers also have a "halo" of being positive, progressive, selfless and fearless above their head. Such views and methods that have been taken for granted makes the following possibility a reality. Some people, in the name of reform, put their own personal preferences and motivations above the interests of the organization. Dignified in form but insincere in substance, they act unscrupulously, outrageously express their preferences, deprive others of their interests to consolidate private rights, get rid of dissidents, and seek personal gains, but legitimize and rationalize their behaviors in the name of organizational interests. This phenomenon requires special vigilance in a transitional society where power is hardly constrained and balanced.

Although responsibility for reform is not only a matter of individuals, reform cannot achieve success without the leadership of individuals. Reform often encounters a variety of resistances because it inevitably requires redistributing power, adjusting organizational structure, resources allocation, and organizational operational procedures, breaking the original habits and order accompanied by higher level of uncertainty. Therefore, reform calls for strong leadership from its promoters. According to Burns's definition, leadership refers to the process in which people with specific motives and purposes mobilize various institutional, political, and psychological resources to stimulate, attract and satisfy followers' motives in the process of competing and conflicting with others. The important foundation for leading and driving the reform process is power. Power includes two basic elements, namely, motives and resources. The two elements are interrelated and mutually reinforcing. Without motives, the value of resources will decrease with weaker power, and motives will be worthless without resources to guarantee its realization.

Why have powers been resisted or challenged since the ancient times? The primary reason is that the motives of the power holder fails to represent or reflect the needs of the organization and organizational members. The secondary reason is the lack of resources controlled by power-holders.

The nature of power is a type of relationship, which is the interaction between power holders with specific motivates, resources and the objects of power with specific motives and resources. The power base of both sides, which is the asymmetry of the inspirational power of motives and morals, and the asymmetry of the owned resources, can lead to an asymmetry in the interaction and influential powers between the two sides. As a result, one side can influence and dominate the behaviors of the other side, even deprive the other side of their will.

By emphasizing that power is by nature a "relationship" rather than a "thing" such as a crown, an imperial jade seal, a gun, or a physical object that can be directly passed on or inherited, we intend to convey the message that the reformer who obtains legal power and the position to issue orders only possesses part of the power foundation. To truly consolidate his power, one must seriously consider the needs of the power objects and carefully cultivate and manage the relationship. At the same time, reformers must scrupulously assess the internal and external environment where organizations conduct reform, as well as their resources and capabilities so as to develop appropriate reform strategies.

Do Not Be a Lonely Reformer

What the reformer should first clearly understand is that reform is never a personal matter. Reformers can have a lonely inner world, but they must have appeal for a broad group of followers. It will not take too long for a reformer who plays the role of a lone ranger to lose his courage and confidence, which will be replaced by inner loneliness and bewilderment during the process of strategic reform. At the same time, loneliness and bewilderment often severely erode their sense of security, making their reforming behaviors more self-protecting, and even more narrow-minded.

Therefore, before reformers begin to initiate an important reform, they must first understand a question, "How do most organizational members and key external stakeholders understand my motives for the reform?" If most people believe that the reform is for private interests, such as placing trusted followers in a certain position, getting rid of dissidents, and seeking personal gains, the reformer needs to think again about whether to launch this reform.

What the reformer views on their true motives for the reform may be important to himself, but it does not make much sense for organizational members to participate in and support the reform. Throughout the ages, all dictators firmly believe in their own senses of justice, morality, responsibility and purpose, such as Qin Shi Huang and Hitler. To take a step back, reformers still face risks if they can't make the majority of followers correctly understand their lofty motives.

Second, the motives of reformers cannot be directly observed. In high-tech enterprises, rational organizational members and external key stakeholders do not identify the reformers' motives by simply listening to what they say, but more by observing the actions and measures taken by reformers. In the process of observing the reformers' actions and identifying their motives, organizational members will pay particular attention to the way reformers deal with their own interests, and the interests of small groups closely related to them. Some reformers often face a dilemma due to this situation: even if the reformer is willing to exercise forbearance and make some sacrifices to demonstrate their just motives, they might make deals with certain organizational members to obtain a leadership position, which can result in a small interest group. After the reformer becomes the leader, if he is eager to fulfill his promise, most organizational members may doubt their motives; if he fails to honor his promise, his original supporters will turn into opponents. Thus, the classic line of the film "*Infernal Affairs*" really makes sense — "You shall pay for what you have done." There is always a price to pay if the reformers have a weaker power foundation.

The right motive for reform comes from the goals of organization and the underlying needs of the organizational members. If the reform motives or goals cannot truly reflect the needs of the majority of the organizational members, it just means temporary improved efficiency due to the change of leader. Organizational members will consider them as the audience of this game, having no intention to participate in the reform since it has nothing to do with their interests. It is difficult to act without any justifiable reason. Reformers will find it hard to appeal to a broad group of followers without motives or goals to truly reflect their needs, especially for those people of insight.

Learn to Manage Conflicts

Reformers need to assess whether they possess the essential qualities to become successful reformers.

There is no one image for successful reformers. Some of them are tall and good-looking, and some have plain looks, so we can only identify certain qualities they have in common and some qualities they do not share. In addition to commitment, perseverance, courage, and selflessness, successful reformers also need emotional maturity to restrain themselves. The rage of an ordinary person may only hurt one or several of his neighbors, but the fury of an emotionally-unconstrained CEO can bring disaster to the entire organization. Since it is impossible to carry out reform without any resistance, successful reformers also need to be able to effectively deal with differences, bargain with others, persuade people, and return one's favor properly.

Successful reformers need to pursue mutual realization or joint realization. Maslow sees self-realization as the highest level of need for human beings. However, it is not enough for successful reformers to only pursue self-realization. The pursuit of self-realization is too individual and departmental, which is more suitable for simple personal behavior because it is difficult to evoke the response of followers. Successful reformers need to pursue mutual realization or joint realization. Mutual realization is not achieved through internal factors or fulfilling the needs of the reformer, but through the interaction of the reformers and the organizational members, the open and inclusive attitude of the reformers, and their abilities to draw lessons, learn from the surrounding environment, and to balance autonomy, creativity, and dependence on others.

Therefore, the value of reform success brought by the reformers' personalities is always linked to their motives. If the reformer's goal reflects or represents the needs of the organization itself or most organizational members, his persistence, determination, no-compromise, no-retreat, and fearlessness will become a mental strength to inspire, rally, and motivate followers, as well as a strong cornerstone to achieve the reform success. But if the reformer's goal fails to represent the deep-level value of the organization and the needs of the majority of the organizational members, the above qualities of reformers will turn into signs of being unscrupulous, dictatorial, violent, and cruel. Although he may coerce some organizational members to participate in the reform process, more of his time is spent on performing the "solo dance" in front of the most organizational members who take an indifferent wait-and-see attitude. In such a situation, the reformer will find it hard to keep up appearances in the face of the public's judgement. If the resources controlled by the reformer are strong enough, some profit-seekers within the organization might follow him with applause, acclaim, and flattery to reduce the feelings of loneliness and anxiety to some extent.

Managing conflicts is also an indispensable skill for reformers. Successful reformers always stand above various interest groups when encountering organizational conflicts, and stimulate creative thinking to promote creative transition through constructive task conflicts instead of destructive task conflicts. Poor reformers are always directly involved in organizational conflicts to confront relevant interest groups face-to-face.

In addition, it is certain that reformers who are reform-minded but indecisive, irresolute, and suspicious can barely achieve success.

In addition to motives, moral qualities, and abilities, reformers also need to assess the reform resources they can rely on and take control of, including resources within the organization and resources provided by the external environment. Firstly, to assess the resources within the organization:

- Which groups are supporters of the reform? What are their positions and how much influence they have in the organization? How many are they? How about their loyalty to, and confidence in the reform's success? A large but distracted group that lacks loyalty and determination often create illusions for reformers who might overestimate their strengths, resulting in risks to the reform.
- How many economic resources can the organization use to support the reform? This includes the amount of funds, the information resources, their quality, promptness, controllability, and so on.
- Besides, to assess the available resources in the external environment:
    - o Who is the key external force that has a significant effect on the power or status of the reformer? Who is the key outside force that supports the reformer? What about their position or influence power? How is their recognition or loyalty to the reformer?
    - o What are the key stakeholders of the organization, such as loan banks, suppliers, agents, and so on? How do they agree with and support the reformers and the reform they initiate? Are they willing to provide help at a critical moment? For example, does the bank give loan support; does the supplier give a longer period of time (return period); and is the agent willing to pay the company in advance at crucial time? Or it is the other way around?
- Social public understanding and value orientation. Is the reform value orientation consistent with the public opinion? How does the public

understand the motives of the reformer? Where does public opinion stand on the position of the reformer?

The rational assessment of motives, quality, environment and resources is not intended to make reformers timid and overcautious. Rather, it aims to help reformers more comprehensively assess the risks of reform in order to develop more reliable strategies, which can avoid failures caused by too much idealism and simple mind.

Comment: The Discipline and Punishment of Reformers — Hao Yazhou

As Professor Liu Xue said in the article, reform is a neutral term without personal emotion. Therefore, reform does not always mean a good start, which can be explained by many reforms in China's modern history. However, with the continuous influx of Western revolutionary theories and the deep desire for the reform of the Chinese people after the policy of the reform and opening-up, the term "reform" has been endowed with strong emotion.

Meanwhile, the reformers are also taken to the altar. Indeed, the current era is at a historical turning point of reform where business leaders like using "change" to glorify themselves. The reformer is more like a stock that has been chased up. However, behind the craziness should be the silence of history. For historical reasons, we need to get ourselves out of craziness to evaluate reform and reformers associated with ourselves with rational thinking.

Professor Liu Xue redefines the reformer from the perspective of ideological system. In the past, examination of the character and emotion of the reformers was constrained by reformers themselves, but ignored the relationship between the subject and the object of the reform. This mutual relationship is "power", as emphasized by Liu Xue in this article. It also confirms Michel Foucault's point of view that man is a phenomenon of knowledge, and knowledge is a phenomenon of power.

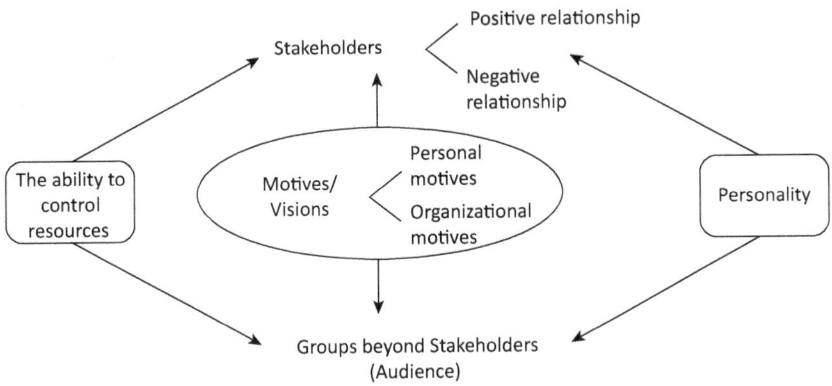

Figure 1 Power/relationship of reformers

In the end, our understanding of society has entered the realm of power and relationships (Figure 1). A company's reform is often reflected in the transfer of power relationships. There is no harm in providing the paradigm of reform from the perspective of power.

As the most pathetic reformer in modern China, Emperor Guangxu and his failure were often interpreted as the result of conservative conspiracy. However, if we re-examine this paradigm of power relationships, we may come to another conclusion: Emperor Guangxu, as a reform leader, was doomed to fail. His failure was inevitable regardless of the grand historical background. He would still fail as an individual organization.

First of all, what were the real motives behind Emperor Guangxu's reforms? The 27-year-old Guangxu was in an age of extreme psychological reactance due to the suppression and manipulation of Empress Dowager Cixi from a young age. According to writer Ma Licheng, the first priority for Guangxu was to get rid of Cixi's manipulation. Therefore, some modern historians believe that the reform is a moral high ground occupied by Guangxu's declaration of war to Cixi.

Second, Guangxu himself did not have the power to control resources. At that time, the sovereign ruler of the Qing government was Cixi, and the resources that Guangxu had access to were limited to intellectuals without political power such as Kang Youwei and Liang Qichao. At the same time, with a strong desire to get rid of Cixi, Guangxu did not take this woman with the highest authority into consideration when balancing his relationship in the beginning, which left an opportunity of the counterattack from Cixi in the future.

Then, Guangxu did not have a good ability to balance relationships. He was too radical in dealing with the relationship between reformists and conservatives. One manifestation was the dismissal of Li Hongzhang, the minister of the Westernization Movement. It was a big mistake that Guangxu removed Li Hongzhang from office just because of his identity as Cixi's minister, because he failed to understand Li Hongzhang's important status in the political pattern of the late Qing Dynasty and Li's deep appeal to organizational reform. The second manifestation was Guangxu's massive and rapid abolishment of the old-generation officials and the great use of reformers, a radical approach that inevitably reduced the prestige of Guangxu among both the court and commoners. "Successful reformers always stand above various interest groups involved in organizational conflicts, and promote the transition of creativity through constructive task conflicts instead of destructive task conflicts, and the stimulation of creative thinking. Poor reformers are always directly involved in organizational conflicts to confront with relevant interest groups face to face."

Of course, the above three aspects cannot fully summarize Guangxu's mistakes, since there are many reasons for the failure of the Hundred Days of Reform. However, from the perspective of Guangxu himself, it is his improper way of dealing with power relationships that makes him eventually a tragic reformer.

Not all reformers are great, even if they are full of pathos. Today, we call for reformers, but we particularly need reformers who can truly internalize organizational goals into the needs of reforms, because they are "able to formulate appropriate strategies based on the internal and external environment organizations face as well as the capabilities and resources of the individual to effectively control the reform process."

About the Author

Liu Xue is Professor in Guanghua School of Management, Peking University. This article was originally published in the 4th issue of *CEIBS Business Review* in 2009.

VII

Does Your Job Match Your Personality? Analysis and Suggestions of Personalities of Chinese Managers

Jean Lee

It is said that your personality is your destiny. A metaphor demonstrates the importance of personalities to individual development. Apparently, having a job whose nature is contradictory to one's personality is like forcing people who are used to writing with their right hand to write with their left hand. We try to use a more scientific tool for personality assessment to inspect Chinese managers and provide reference for their personal development by examining the characteristics of their personality and job.

Through carrying out research on more than 350 Chinese senior managers, we find that the proposition of how manager's personality matches their work is reasonable, but there is much room for improvement. Although the personality has connatural constitution, environment plays quite an important role in transforming people's personality. The personality of Chinese manager group needs to be improved.

Conclusion of Personality Assessment

There are many theories and methods for studying and evaluating personalities. In the 1920s, the DISC Personality Assessment tool created by American Psychologist Dr. William Moulton Marston was proved to have high test validity after being used and verified by more than 30 million people worldwide. We used it to assess the personalities of more than 350 Chinese EMBA students who are senior managers of various organizations in China.

Two behavioral axes are used in DISC. The two ends of the longitudinal axis represent the behavioral tendencies of "arbitrary" and "passive" respectively, which are used to assess whether people respond to the environment proactively or passively. The two ends of the horizontal axis represent "openness" and "restraint" to assess people's different mentalities when interacting with others.

Based on the DISC Behavior Classification System, the four dimensions of personality, dominance, influence, steadiness, and compliance, are shown in Figure 1.

As for the characteristics of the four dimensions of personality, dominance-oriented people deal with affairs straightforwardly with high

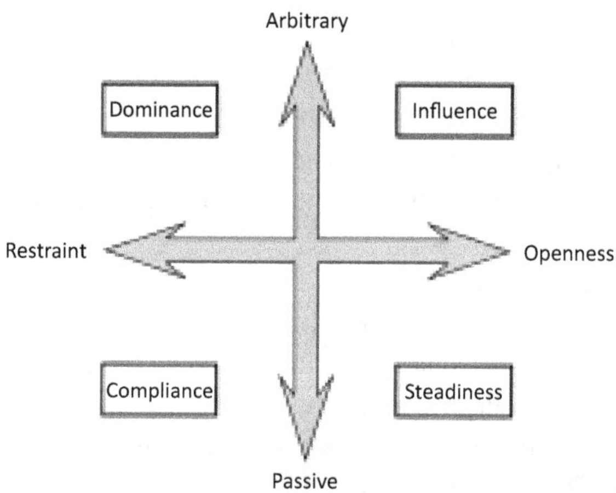

Figure 1 DISC behaviour classification system
Source: CFP Picture Gallery.

standards and strict requirements, desiring to surpass others when they get along with people; influence-oriented people are good at communicating and social intercourse due to their friendly and outgoing characters, behaving with perfect composure in a strange environment; steadiness-oriented people are steady, kind, patient, stubborn, have no interest in change, and have the habit of planning carefully before action; compliance-oriented people are organized, are interested in accuracy and order, and prefer to act according to the rules. The two axes represent the equilibrium of the two personalities on both sides of the axis.

According to the results of the assessment, the most common dimension of personality that Chinese managers share is steadiness, followed by compliance. In contrast, the number of people who are dominance- and influence-oriented is relatively small.

For managers of different levels, among the senior managers and middle-high-level managers exist a majority of steady people and a minority of compliant people; among the middle-level managers exist many compliant people and few dominant people. For different types of organizations, there are a majority of steady managers and few dominant managers in government and government-sponsored institutions, and there are a majority of steady managers, and a minority of influential and compliant managers in private enterprises.

Interestingly, compared with male managers, there is a significantly higher proportion of dominance and influence types among female managers, as well as a considerably lower proportion of steadiness type.

Advice for Chinese Managers

The first step in improving personality is to understand it. The aim of evaluating and analyzing the personality of Chinese managers is to give advice to improve their personality. As long as Chinese managers pay attention to the alignment between their own personalities and job requirements for self-adjustment and improvement, they will surely find a tacit understanding, and feel happy and free in their work.

Emphasis on Personality Adjustment. The inner personality shows the most essential and true self, which reflects one's intrinsic motivation and desire. The external personality is the perceived ideal behaviors based on the requirements of the job position, which reflects people's recognition of work expectations instead of the true self. The personality conversion refers to the difference between the inner personality and work personality of the subject, showing the ongoing personality adjustment of the subject and indicating the pressure from balancing the relationship of two types of personalities.

According to the result of the research, for the majority of the organizational managers, their inner personality outweighs their work personality. 60% of managers are steadier than work expectation; more than 40% of managers show more compliance than work expectation; about 40% of managers show more compliance dominant than job expectation. On the contrary, about 40% of managers have lower level of influence power than job expectation.

Although part of a manager's personality is instinctive, it is more shaped by long-term job roles and requirements. There are no completely improper personalities, which require people to adjust and balance personalities well. It can be said that the gap between a person's inner personality and work personality is the room one has for improvement. Starting from how to do a better job, one can infer the actions one needs to take, based on which one can further infer the personality deficiency one needs to overcome. For example, managers need enhanced ability of communication and social intercourse. Even those managers with compliant personalities can find dominant and influential tendencies in their personality through training.

Surplus of Steadiness Produces the Need to Pick Up Pace. Steadiness is the most popular type of personality among managers, occupying more than half of managers except the mixed personality. Steadiness is not a shortcoming. From the personality perspective, steady managers expect to maintain positive and mutually supportive interpersonal relationships, are willing to support their peers, eager to avoid conflicts and confrontations, and desire interpersonal harmony. From the perspective of teamwork, the existence of a large number of managers is critical to team stability and harmony, which is the pursuit of many organizations. The problem is that steady managers don't like abrupt changes or disturbances, and it takes time and patience for them to adapt to new situations, resulting in a passive and negative feeling they show to others in a rapidly changing environment. In the current environment for Chinese organizations, it is true that making a blind decision is not desirable, but failing to keep pace with the times will also lead to failure and dying out.

We recommend that managers in the dimension of steadiness pick up their pace in the face of change by way of consciously adding more work partners accustomed to fast paces of work when establishing leadership teams to absorb more proactive and enterprising insights.

The Lack of Influential Managers Calls for Attention to Harmony. Organizational decision makers should fully consider the different characteristics of managers when setting up their management team. Chinese managers aspiring for self-improvement should cultivate their own influence-oriented personality tendencies.

Compared to the great number of steadiness-oriented managers, managers belonging to influence dimension are particularly scarce. The scarcity not only refers to its small number, but also shows the importance of this type of managers who are critical mediators in creating a harmonious working atmosphere. Influence-oriented managers are friendly and cordial, considering the participation in social activities and building positive relationships with others as the most important thing. Of course, they might neglect work due to paying too much attention to relationship-building, or shirk their responsibilities under too much pressure.

On the one hand, the lack of influence-dimension managers shows that the current atmosphere in the organization puts emphasis on responsibility and work. On the other hand, it also demonstrates the relatively dull way of working among managers. After all, maintaining a certain proportion of influence-oriented managers is the key to a harmonious work-place relationship and an embodiment of the organization's humanistic care. It is necessary to consider whether there is a relaxed and harmonious atmosphere in the current Chinese manager team who focuses more on work than humanity.

Moderation to be Improved, Quality and Efficiency to be Balanced. Dominant managers like control and power, regardless of the situation, they will manage to take control of the entire operation, with little tolerance for challenges to their dominance. The cultural tradition, "a man of virtue should be temperate, kindhearted, respectful, thrifty and modest," has made the dominant management style unpopular in China. More than 70% of the managers studied in this research show moderate level in the dimension of dominance. They are neither extreme commanders nor complete obedient people, showing a "moderate" trend, in consistence with the Chinese traditional education and social customs. The moderation doctrine reflects both the mentality to make progress and the avoidance of aggressiveness. It balances advancing and retreating, implying the meaning of "mature" in Chinese tradition.

Any job is matched with appropriate personality. About 20% of managers think that his position is expected to show a higher level of dominance, and about 30% of managers think that their position should show less dominance. Therefore, there is still room for improvement in the managers' dominance dimension considering their moderation tendency, because a more distinctive personality that matches the job position can reduce communication costs and improve management efficiency.

Compliance-oriented managers tend to study the detailed materials and technical details, hoping to explore the problems in implementation and maintenance that managers of other personalities may overlook. They are trustworthy as they only accept reliable proposals and acquire detailed information. But they may be disadvantaged by their overly rigorous nature and the lack of efficiency. Nowadays, the internal compliance of organizational managers is moderately high, and almost no managers show low level of internal compliance. More than 40% of managers are inherently more compliant than work expectations, and 20% of managers are inherently less compliant than job expectations, indicating the unreasonableness of fit degree between managers' personality and their work. While most people work too meticulously and inefficiently, there are some managers whose rigorousness and work efficiency fail to meet job requirements. We recommend that managers properly adjust the relationship between work rigorousness and timeliness to achieve a dynamic balance between quality and efficiency.

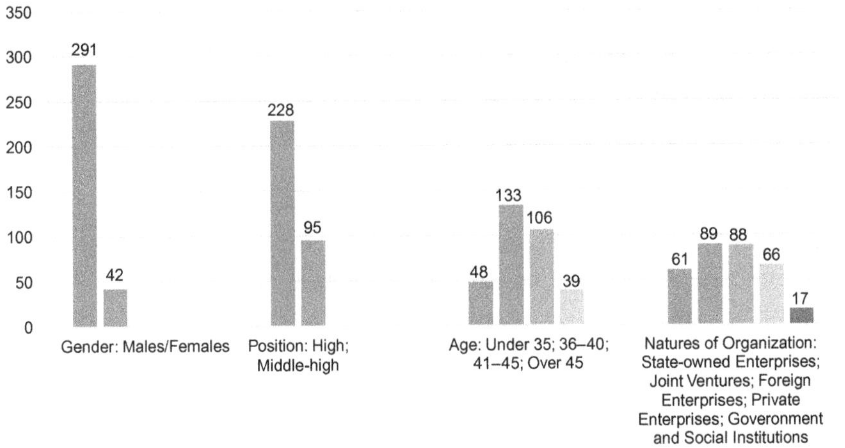

Figure 2 Descriptive statistics of the characteristics of the subject

Managers in Chinese Enterprises Should Take More Initiative. The differences of managers' personality in different industries can be considered as a very interesting phenomenon, which shows the differences of organizational culture and climate in different industries, as well as the essential role of the environment in shaping individual personalities.

According to the research result (the characteristics of objects in this test are shown in Figure 2), compared with the managers in Chinese organizations, managers from foreign enterprises and joint ventures are slightly better in terms of initiative. There is a larger proportion of managers of dominance and influence in foreign enterprises. A high proportion of high-initiative personalities also implies a cultural atmosphere that emphasizes individuality, which is subconsciously influenced by the organizational culture as a natural choice of managers.

This is where Chinese managers should learn with a modest attitude. Explicit personality can simplify the internal relationship of the organization, reduce the communication cost, and display emotions and even conflicts openly in workplace to improve work efficiency.

Managers from private enterprises show a high proportion in the steadiness dimension, accounting for more than 40%. Through the analysis of their positions, the research finds that the proportion of chairmen and general managers (including senior vice presidents) are fifty-fifty among steadiness-oriented managers. Since these managers pursue interpersonal harmony and strive to avoid conflicts, they like to plan carefully before taking action and dislike abrupt changes in the environment. It can be considered that the mid- and senior-level professional managers in private enterprises tend to pursue stability and strive for security, but lack the ability to cope with environmental changes. As far as personality is concerned, they are good at maintaining their predecessors' achievements, but poor at pioneering new areas.

Females are as Excellent as Their Male Colleagues. There are many successful businesswomen who are as excellent as their male colleagues. In terms of their personality, good at communication and building a harmonious relationship is one factor for their success. The study finds that the proportion of influence-oriented managers among females is more than double that of influence-oriented managers among males.

It is a natural advantage for women to "use softness to overcome hardness". Meanwhile, female managers are also changing people's traditional views with a significantly higher proportion of dominance-oriented managers by using masculine approach for management, and showing stronger position and more aggressiveness, as well as absolute authority and control to their subordinates and work. All of these show that the success of female managers not only requires their full play to the softness advantage, but also the adjustment of "feminine" style to adopt a strong style to balance their leadership qualities.

Because women have been in a disadvantaged position for a long time, it is not easy for them to fight in the business world. Women tend to be more self-aware in their struggles and more consciousness to overcome their own deficiencies, including the improvement of their personality structure. Such awareness of female managers is worth learning by male managers.

About the Author

Jean Lee, Ph.D., is Michelin Leader and Human Resources chaired professor of CEIBS, Director of the Management Department, and Director of the Leadership Behavior Experiment Center in CEIBS. Her main areas of research include leadership, corporate culture and female management. Her best-selling books include *Great Men's Sons Seldom Do Well*, *Organizational Behavior*, *China Market Leadership* and so on. This article was originally published in the 5th issue of *CEIBS Business Review* in 2008.

VIII

How does the Board of Directors Manage the "CEO Turnover Plan"?

Li Yang

In August 2008, the Fortune website listed the "Top Ten CEOs in the hot seat in the United States". Under the background of the subprime crisis and the skyrocketing oil price, the CEOs of Lehman Brothers, Fannie Mae and Freddie Mac were among the top three, closely followed by Washington Mutual, Merrill Lynch, General Motors, and SiriusXM Radio. The last three CEOs were Howard Schultz from Starbucks, Jeff Immelt from General Electric, and Yang Zhiyuan from Yahoo.

There are good reasons that these CEOs are resented. For example, regarding the top three CEOs in the list, their salaries in 2007 were US$40 million, US$11.7 million, and US$18.3 million respectively, but the company's shareholders lost US$26 billion, US$52 billion, and US$36 billion in comparison.

The people in the hot seats are not only the star CEOs at the brunt of the wind and the tip of the wave. In this era of great change, CEOs, no matter from industry giants or hidden champions, North America or Asia, manufacturing enterprises or service companies, are always the focuses under huge pressure from all sides. The in-executive CEOs are the first to be blamed when the stock price and the company have major problems.

It Takes Great Risks and Responsibilities to Replace the CEO

Every director should be concerned about whether a company has a competent CEO.

Face the reality, and give up the ostrich policy. Change is part of life, and drastic changes can happen without early warning signals. For example, a newly appointed CEO can be fired, and a CEO who has worked for many years can be asked to make way or retire.... It is hard to predict when CEOs will leave their jobs. On the other hand, what if the CEO is killed by a truck tomorrow? There should be a contingency plan for a bizarre idea like a "truck test".

The company is likely to get into trouble if the board of directors is not fully prepared before the crisis erupts, such as the identification of the candidate of the new CEO. In 2002, the CEO of the TRW Company in the United States suddenly resigned, leaving the board of directors at a loss since they did not have a turnover candidate within the organization. In three days, the board received a takeover request from Northrop Grumman and had to compromise with the decision.

In contrast, the board of directors at McDonald's is much more powerful. In 2004, the CEO Jim Cantalupo suddenly resigned, and the board of directors convened to appoint Charlie Bell to take over as CEO within a few hours. The procedure shows McDonald's strength.

In any case, the change of CEOs has a huge impact on the company and its shareholders. Dealing with CEO turnover is one of the most difficult tasks for the board. It will be a more serious crisis to find a satisfactory candidate at critical moments. The company should find the successor in time and control the turnover process, regardless of why the former CEO left the company. This is not a talent show, but a journey to search and care for the future helmsman.

There are many examples of successful CEO turnovers. In 1993, IBM chose the "layman" Guo Shina as a new CEO in the risk of falling behind Prime, DEC and Wang An. He finally laid the foundation for strategic transformation, which was referred to as "Leading Elephants to Dance". The board of directors of IBM was considered to "benefit the company for decades". Many other companies also not only have excellent CEOs, but also a great team of CEOs, such as General Electric, Emerson Electric, Procter & Gamble, Colgate, Unilever, CitiBank, General Food, Kraft....

There are lots of bad examples too. Due to the retailer Kmart's repeated mistakes of choosing three improper CEOs in eight years, Walmart took the chance to overtake Kmart and leave them behind. The consecutive three wrong choices of CEO in Apple Computer also led to struggling days for this company.

Among Chinese enterprises, the power substitution of Wangke and Yuliang in Vanke Group was considered to be a relatively successful one. Other successful CEOs include Yang Yuanqing of Lenovo Group, Jin Zhiguo of Tsingtao Brewery, and Wang Jiafen of Bright Dairy. Of course, there are many unsuccessful examples and some of them may be incomprehensible. For example, China's telecom giants have exchanged positions through the game of "Musical Chairs" several times, which is beyond the business logic.

In general, with a short history and complex environment, domestic companies have drawn more lessons but had fewer experiences to share in CEO turnover compared with marketing activities.

Five Principles of CEO Turnover Plan

Since the CEO is an important and risky position, how should the board think ahead and plan carefully?

In the "CEO Turnover Report" issued by the National Association of Corporate Directors, RHR International has made contributions to the selection and evaluation of CEO candidates. The RHR recommends that the turnover plan take the following five principles into consideration.

The CEO turnover plan must be based on a strategic replacement plan. It should be with the aim of not just selecting the next CEO, but seeking the best solutions to making the company's strategic decisions and finding the ideal candidate to implement the strategy to enhance the company's competitiveness.

The goal of turnover is to find the right leader at the right time. Many boards of directors select CEOs based on their past performances. It is easy to consider past success as a guarantee for future performance, but this method provides incomplete information to make decisions.

First of all, someone who has a successful experience in a specific industry is not necessarily suitable for the new CEO position. Secondly, using past performance as the main criterion to select a CEO fails to take into account the company's future needs and the candidate's capacity to adapt to specific challenges, including industry changes, company situation, competitive position and company culture.

Successful turnover requires cooperation with current CEO. The turnover of CEO is one of the most important issues facing the board of directors in serving the interests of shareholders.

In the past, the CEO chose his own successor who would be approved by the board of directors. The unsuccessful examples of CEO turnover imply the dangers of this approach. The selection of a new CEO requires cooperation with the current CEO, and the board has the ultimate responsibility. In addition, the board's responsibility not only lies in examining the current CEO or selecting a successor. More importantly, the board is responsible for making a proper long-term plan to maintain leadership continuity.

CEO turnover is an ongoing process. It is a common phenomenon that, after the boards find a new CEO, they forget to arrange the subsequent selection process and the reserves of potential CEO candidates until the next re-selection or crisis reminds them of the turnover problem again.

General Electric spent ten years looking for the successor of Jack Welch. One of the reasons why JP Morgan Chase acquired First Bank in 2004 was to have its CEO Jamie Dimon as the successor of William Harrison, the then-CEO of Morgan Chase. The board should have a long-term plan for CEO turnover.

The board of directors should encourage and improve the talent pool. A company must have "inventory", and a good turnover plan is helpful to build a rich talent pool and improve the selection criteria for a specific period. "Inventory" can help the board of directors accomplish a task with ease. In 2000, the board of directors in P&G asked Jagger, the shortest-lived CEO, to leave and hired A.G. Lavelli as the new CEO. The success of the company proved that the board's ability to correct the mistaken decision was of great value.

The assessment plans of most companies are often useless, unless they include ongoing plans for talent development. One of the hallmarks of a well-run company is the development of the management team within the organization. It is no coincidence that companies specializing in management, including GE, Hewlett-Packard, and Federal Signal Corporation, are known for their talent pools.

The Board Should Clarify the Company's Needs

It's hard to put into practice what is known. Principle will buy no meal. The board needs to do some homework in terms of the CEO turnover.

The fundamental issue of the turnover plan is to find a CEO that matches the company's strategy. The CEO must be able to accept the current and future challenges facing the company, and handle the compensation and performance appraisal. RHR recommends that the board of directors first clarify the following three aspects:

Organizational Strategy. Based on the company's strategic review, the boards should ask themselves a few key questions: What must be done for the company's success? What changes are the industry experiencing? How does the market competitiveness affect the company? In other words, what is the key issue to a company's success? What are the company's requirements on culture to achieve the business strategy?

The above issue requires cooperation with the current CEO. In March 2004, David Smith, the CEO of Global Medical Corporation with US$1.3 billion in assets, even set up a department to communicate with the board regarding strategic issues. The boards of other companies have also urged CEOs to hire consultants to independently evaluate company strategies.

Factors for CEO's success. The board must ask the CEO: How should we work hard to achieve the key aspects of the strategy? To concretely implement this step, the board of directors should clearly define the CEO's work and the success elements, including leadership and core ideas.

For example, for a company whose development strategy is transferred into acquisition, its requirements for managers' abilities will change dramatically. To succeed in the new environment, CEOs must have leadership skills and capabilities to shape a culture that fosters collaboration — a big difference from running an independent company.

The "post-acquisition" stage is another thing. In 2001, the board of directors of Bank of America began to re-select the CEO. Since the drastic acquisition made by the then-CEO made Bank of America the largest consumer bank in the United States, the board's attention was focused on the capabilities to integrate resources. Finally, Kenneth Lewis was selected. He suspended the crazy acquisition, but worked on consolidating foundation, market segmentation, and cross-selling. It was not until 2003 that the Bank of America resumed large-scale acquisitions.

The requirements on the behaviors of new leaders. The challenges facing the company hold significance for senior leadership. The key quality of a CEO candidate is not how well he/she behaves elsewhere, but whether he/she can handle the new job in a new environment. The boards should ask themselves: what kind of people does the company need? What value matters? Does this candidate suit the current culture of the company — or should the culture be changed? The boards also need to pay attention to the candidate's personal qualities, values, and development needs.

There will be disastrous results if the board chooses the wrong CEO. Little Walter Connolly, CEO of New England Bank in Boston, was known for his iron fists named three "W"s: Whatever Walter Wants. The result was the company becoming a group of yes-men who were extremely afraid of him. Behind the iron fist was the US$1.2 billion in bad debts brought by Connolly's oversight and dereliction of duty. When the board fired him, the bank was also closed down by the federal government.

Differences of Leadership in Four Types of Companies

The clarification of the company's needs by the board is followed by the evaluation of the candidate.

A good candidate should have the qualities needed to be a successful CEO. According to experiences accumulated over more than 50 years, the experts at RHR put forward some universal characteristics shared by successful CEOs in different corporate cultures and environments (Table 1).

Still, it is not enough for the company to find an ideal CEO using just universal characteristics. Challenges and goals must be considered: How can the company keep a foothold in the market? Which development phase is the company in? What is the strategic intention and how is it manifested?

Table 1: Characteristics of Successful CEOs

Personality	Behavior
Problem-Solving Ability	• Be clever and flexible • Have good judgment and insight • Ability to focus on key issues
Disposition and Incentives Factors	• A sound mind • Uphold personal values and business values • Use power cautiously
Interpersonal Relations and Communication	• Communicate with others efficiently • Ability to manage supporters both inside and outside the company • Consistently articulate and adhere to the principle from the company's perspective
The Understanding of Yourself and Others	• Be aware of your strengths and weaknesses • Have a thorough understanding of the needs of organizations and others
Characteristics of Leadership	• Outline the blueprint of reform • Provide planning steps for reform and carefully implement them • Express recognition and concern for others • Clearly express the expected value • Become a trustworthy good example • Identify the company's value agenda • Develop and promote the talent team

Based on the complex reality, RHR summarizes four types of companies in terms of the leadership skills and performance that CEOs should have in specific situations (Table 2). These four types of companies include:

- **Rapid growth**: Companies experiencing rapid growth in both benefits and market share, with the launch of new products or the development of new markets;
- **Turning point**: Companies who are suddenly experiencing trouble, and thus have major financial needs and require operational adjustments;
- **Merger and integration**: Two companies which face the problem of resource integration and operation; and

Table 2. Core Leadership Differences of the Four Types of Enterprises

Company situation	Core leadership factors
Rapid Growth	• Have an eye for alternatives outside of tradition and convention • Calmly meet the challenge • Communicate effectively and be clear to the future • Have necessary talents around • Power of authorization: Trust others to complete the work
Turning Point	• Regular gatherings with long-term consideration • Stand one's ground in the face of conflict • Clear and concise communicators • Encourage people to think about the company's future rather than the past • Establish a united team under the new agenda
Merger and Acquisition	• Present the organization's blueprint • Understand the potential implications of the two organizations' cultures and their differences • Recognize that culture is more powerful than individuals and be able to work under cultural differences • Reach a consensus on building management model
Industry with Structural Changes	• Excellent industry knowledge • Divergent thinking • Ready to accept either course • Passion for change • Establish crisis awareness • Encourage others to think in someone else's position and change management operations

- **Industry change**: Companies belonging to an industry that has experienced major changes, which requires the company to change its culture.

Nobody is perfect. It is not that the CEO has to possess all the good qualities listed above to be successful. But the company should match its strategic needs with the CEO's ability and quality. Certain characteristics and personality traits can help some CEOs perform better.

All in all, the goal of CEO turnover is to find the right person at the right time. Finding the right CEO is the core and most critical issue for the board of directors. This is a long-term process that includes planning, ongoing work, and cooperation with the current CEOs to establish leadership that matches the company's strategic goals.

About the Author

Li Yang is editor of *CEIBS Business Online*. This article was originally published in the 9th issue of *CEIBS Business Review* in 2008.

IX

Feng Lun: "I am Zero"

Zhu Qiong

When it comes to occasions when a galaxy of entrepreneurs gather together, Feng Lun, chairman of Wantong Group, is a frequent participant. But he is usually not the ostentatious one. "As long as someone makes a speech, I will do nothing but to give my full applause." Feng Lun explained this behavior with a sly humour, "Excellent entrepreneurs are my teachers. 'A great teacher produces a brilliant student.' I would like to follow these great teachers and learn from them for free."

As the boss of a well-known real estate group, why does Feng Lun keep a low profile? "According to ancients, the reason why water is wide lies in its low position to pool many things together." Feng Lun believes that lots of experiences and warnings from many "teachers" on different occasions have helped him make few major mistakes during the past two decades of running his business.

Feng Lun, who has devoted himself to studying history and philosophy since middle school, has always used his philosophical thinking from the historical perspective. "Those who believe that they have experienced a series of changes and grown from 0 to 1, from 1 to 100 are underestimating history and time. Human beings are insignificant in the vast universe and the long river of history. I think I am actually nothing, just a "zero".

"Washington-Style" Abdication

It might be easy for Feng Lun to position himself as a "zero" outside the Wantong Group, but it is a difficult task to consider himself as a "zero" within the company. During the nearly 20 years of Wantong's history, Feng is the only one of the six founders who has stayed with the company, which makes him a legendary super authority.

"Many founders have closed the door to forward the development of the company due to their limitations on vision, experience and physical conditions." Feng Lun was aware of the drawbacks of the founder's authority long ago. Through the study of Chinese private enterprises in the past 100 years, he found that the reason why the life cycle of most enterprises is not longer than 15 years was the limitation of the target ceiling identified by the founders consciously or unconsciously. One of the best ways to break the ceiling and live longer than the life cycle is for the founders to abdicate, especially for those private enterprises with a history of 15 to 20 years.

Feng Lun believes that there are two methods for a founder to abdicate. One is the natural abdication adopted by Mao Zedong, and the other is the Washington-style abdication, a method whereby the leader makes early plans to leave and solidifies his values in the form of a constitutional system. By doing this, although Washington abdicated early, his philosophy and values have still worked. Feng Lun chose the second method.

Over the years, Feng Lun has spent a lot of energy on the corporate governance structure and system, as well as cultural construction. Instead of turning Wantong into a carriage that only he could drive, he wants the company to become a car driven by core values, systems and regulations. "Acting according to the rules makes everyone a driver."

With the evolution of the "turning Wantong from a carriage into a car", Feng Lun has abdicated step by step. On August 24, 2009, Feng Lun wrote, "Recently, I have experienced some changes in the way of working and living. Although I am quite busy, I seem to spend most time pursuing uncertain things.... Now I have more time to see the corners of the world, to discuss with God about various thoughts. In short, I am gradually leaving Wantong. This is good, allowing me to have a chance to look at Wantong up and down."

Returning to Zero Wins a Future

The calm Feng Lun contrasts with the entrepreneurs who have encountered the development bottleneck of discontinuity. This kind of calmness benefits from his habits of doing important but not urgent things so as to use the future to guide today's business.

Wantong's business transition to the US model is a future-oriented move. Around 2004, when other companies were busy buying land reserve resources, Wantong was freeing itself from land dependence and transitioning from the Hong Kong model to the US model.

The so-called Hong Kong model is to take responsibility for the entire process of real estate development, which is the positioning strategy used by most real estate companies today; the US model is to hand over all the procedures to professional companies and take responsibility for integrating resources to become housing suppliers and service providers. Obviously, the US model requires companies to make great efforts in product and service management and brand promotion, which is a great challenge for real estate companies that are accustomed to their comfortable zones. However, Feng Lun believes that, since China's land resources will become as limited or even rare as those of some developed countries in the long run, it takes great financial risks to rely on the possession of land resources in the real estate development model, which can easily turn developers into profit-oriented businesses rather than growth-oriented enterprises. Such a developer, in Feng Lun's view, is tantamount to a frog in warm water, which is comfortable now but dangerous in the future.

By studying the real estate industry in the United States and other Asian countries and regions, Feng Lun perceives that the value of the real estate industry is shifting from the development to operation and then to financial management, all the way up to the upstream section of the industrial chain. In other words, real estate developers are becoming the least valuable part of the value chain with the weakest voice. Therefore, it is an inevitable measure for enterprises to climb upstream to be bigger and stronger. In this way, real estate developers are like China's manufacturing industry trying to get rid of the model of manufacturing for other companies and focus on its own brand and R&D.

In order to support the "US model", Feng Lun has made a few precautions. First, invite Tianjin TEDA with the state-owned background to become a shareholder, making Wantong a private and state-owned mixed-ownership enterprise, which lays the foundation for building a domestic high-end brand and financing in the future. Second, enter Manhattan market, the US, and rent "China Center" in 1 World Trade Center to operate it as the overseas office and experimental site for the US model. Third, invest in product development like high-tech companies. In February 2010, Wantong released new products of green eco-residential houses, and announced that new products will be launched every spring. "By taking such measures day by day, our products will be superior than our competitors, and our brand will be accepted like Apple in the electric product market." Feng Lun expects that Wantong to become a high-end brand with cultural connotations.

What's more, Feng Lun also "read" China Taiwan by bike a few months ago. Recently, he invited several professors from Taiwan to teach him about the history and current situation of the region. The purpose of these moves is to strengthen the allocation of resources in Taiwan. "Taiwan enjoys a relatively great degree of marketization and large space for doing business. There are great professional teams and experiences in Taiwan's service industry." Therefore, in addition to doing business in the United States, Feng Lun also attempts to combine the advantages of the market of mainland China with those of Taiwan's market to further realize its strategy to "localize hard resource configuration, globalize soft resource configuration." At present, Wantong's management team has more than 10 members from the US and 10 members from Taiwan.

According to a recent speech delivered by Economist Zhou Qiren, "Chinese private enterprises need to be adept in participating in global competition to effectively use the soft resources brought by the gap of current global development." Hearing this, Feng Lun said with a smile, "We unintentionally did the right thing again."

Non-Contention Lasts

"I am zero, which means I am not a fan of contending with others. So I get along with others in a simple but lasting way." Feng Lun not only pursues this simple philosophy in his life, but also in governing enterprises.

The method of Feng Lun's "running a business in a simplified way" is to do positive things and avoid negative things. The core value he gives to Wantong is simply several words — "Act positively, think creatively for extraordinary performance."

The so-called "positive" is the main rules, trend, certain events and legal system; and "extraordinary performance" requires companies to combine reality, make constant improvement for development and innovation. In Feng Lun's view, the core value reflects the deepest-level judgment of right and wrong as well as choice of good and bad made by a company, especially its leaders. If the core value becomes an unshakable "divine mandate" over time, it will become a core competitiveness, the most imitative and irreplaceable ability of the enterprise.

Wantong's core value was officially presented on August 21, 2009, but Feng Lun said that it existed long ago in the form of "corporate culture".

The vision of "act positively, think creatively for extraordinary performance," is to "take the world as its own responsibility, create wealth and improve oneself based on the interests of enterprises." This is the belief held by Feng Lun when he started his business. However, the ability to convert this belief into the core value was obtained by Feng Lun from Wang Luguang, the former Chief Supervisor of Wantong's board of supervisors.

In 1992, Feng Lun invited Wang Luguang to establish the board of supervisors. Wang Luguang said, "I can help you, but you must 'act positively, think creatively for extraordinary performance.'" The private enterprises at that time had almost no awes and fears, which might make them defy every law and regulation. However, Feng Lun had a "Buddha" around him, Wang Luguang, a disabled person in a wheelchair. Every time Feng Lun talked to him who always sat in a chair, Feng Lun felt that he was talking to a "Buddha". Feng Lun later recalled, "Every time he talks to me, he can enlighten me on a few things. I discuss with him in terms of important issues every time before meeting the board. This is the reason why I avoid making mistakes. He even becomes the reason for me and the enterprise to live on."

Establish Corporate Religion

It is improper for core values to only stay at the corporate executive level. How can they be internalized as a guide for all employees? Feng Lun believes that this is similar to establishing a religion. Religion should firstly have a founding myth to solve the legitimacy problem of "where are you from." Wantong proceeded to solve this problem in 2002 by setting up a historical exhibition hall to conveying the story of the company's origins to its employees.

In addition, religions need scriptures such as the *Bible* and the *Qur'an* so that they can use various stories to preach. In addition to telling stories to employees through the historical exhibition hall, Wantong re-published the "*Wantong Book*" that records the company's history. In addition, the company conveys its culture through various printed or electronic magazines like "*Wantong*", "*Living Home*", and "*Wind Horse Ox*".

Further, religions need places of worship such as churches and temples. In addition to the "sacred hall" for historical exhibition, Wantong also established Longshan School on August 21, 2009 to pass on the corporate culture. Special occasions like the Introspection Day and the New Year's Day have become rituals for Wantong to preach.

This long, accumulating internalization process, in Feng Lun's view, is like making pickles, which slowly ferments the cabbage into sauerkraut. "It takes about one or two generations to stabilize the process."

The inheritance of Wantong's values began as early as their Introspection Day. The company was founded on September 13, 1991. From the second year onwards, the "birthday" has become their "Introspection Day", a day to reflect on what has been done wrong in the past year, or what needs to be strengthened. This rigid annual reflection has been in place for 18 years. Feng Lun will participate in the event in person every year, no matter how busy he is.

"Is introspection useful or not? It might be useless in 1 day or 1 year, and brings a little change in 3 years. But it will definitely be useful in 18 years, and 36 years. Repeatedly doing one simple thing for a long time and take it seriously, you can make a difference." This is almost what Feng Lun must deliver to his employees at the Introspection Day every year.

Feng Lun has a reason to emphasize the significance of the Introspection Day. Several major strategic adjustments and improvements in the history of Wantong are based on the reflections on this day. For example, when Wantong was in a serious crisis before 1996, employees calmed down to reflect on the reasons on this day. After full discussion, everyone realized that the "short-period loan and long-term investment" model in the past was the root reason. After finding the problem, the company began to sell a large number of assets, reduce loans, and retract the investment to focus on the real estate industry. After four years of radical reform, by the year 2000, Wantong had passed the crisis.

The establishment of Wantong's corporate social responsibility system also originated from the Introspection Day three years ago. At that time, the concept of corporate social responsibility started to get popular, but what did it mean for the enterprise? How to fulfill the responsibility? These questions were raised and discussed repeatedly at the introspection meeting. Finally, everyone agreed to establish a system to fulfill the CSR. Therefore, Wantong established an independent public welfare fund, which stipulated that 0.5% to 1% of the company's annual profits would be fixedly donated to the public welfare fund. In addition, employees were required to participate in a four-day paid charity event in which all executives' speech remuneration must be donated to the charity fund.

Wantong not only used many methods to instill its core values, but also relied on the system assessment to ensure implementation and correct errors. For example, Wantong's executives are subject to ethical audits every year. Since 2010, the proportion of ordinary managers' values in their performance evaluation has also increased. If the manager has any records of non-compliance, their grade will not look good even if they reach the performance indicator. Wantong had a similar assessment before, but the proportion is not this large. It is the result of Feng Lun's learning from Ma Yun as Alibaba have the same system.

"Trust makes things simple." Ma Yun's statement at the 10th anniversary of Alibaba's founding was also regarded as a classic by Feng Lun. And he went on to say, "Simple things last."

"Zero can be nothing, or everything." Feng Lun, who considers himself as a zero, actually hopes everything to be long-lasting.

About the Author

Zhu Qiong was a former senior reporter for the *CEIBS Business Review*. This article was originally published in the 5th issue of *CEIBS Business Review* in 2010.

X

Joining a Time-Honored Enterprise: My Days in Tata Steel

B. Muthuraman

The Best Leadership Trait is Humility

Someone once asked me, what kind of leadership was needed to take control of a company like Tata Steel with a long history? What are the differences from managing an emerging IT company in India?

In my opinion, there is no difference at all. The management of both emerging companies and traditional business require leadership. In fact, I really don't like the name of "traditional business". For a company that existed for hundreds of years, what it is at present has great differences from what it was 20 years ago, because the company must be more modern-oriented to adapt to the environment, whether in terms of technology, ways of thinking, or business processes management. In a sense, controlling an emerging and fast-growing company is not the biggest challenge. It might take bigger challenges to lead a traditional mature business which does not have many growth opportunities at all times.

The leadership trait that I value most is humility, because it is often an important dividing line between good leaders and great leaders. Without humility, it is difficult to grow from good leaders into great leaders. In addition, leadership is also about the "crazy" pursuit of success. The wisdom in making decisions and the art of motivation are also important factors in leadership.

Worldwide, currently there is an obvious tendency of "packaging leadership", a method used by leaders to make themselves best-sellers to cater to certain popular standards. However, in my opinion, true leaders need to return to the fundamentals to be more genuine, and be able to establish sustainable business instead of only attempting to attract the attention from the public. Many companies mentioned in Jim Collins' management books are unfamiliar names, let alone the leaders behind them. It is therefore essential to recognize that the main purpose of the "packaging leadership" tendency and flamboyant companies is attracting the attention of the media and the public to a large extent. For Tata Steel, we will continue to do what we should do, without caring for external evaluation.

Make 40,000 Arrows Pointing into the Same Target

Tata Steel's domestic company in India has the lowest operating cost of all the global steel enterprises. We have a set of mature procedures and approaches to lower the cost.

No best but only better. Our philosophy of operation is continuous improvement, which is reflected in many areas. Tata Steel has established processes in human resources management, production, marketing, sales, finance, training, and other aspects. However, all the industries and enterprises have a same basic process. The difference is that processes cannot be completed without people, leaving a huge room for improvement.

We have three steps to optimize the process. First, standardize the process; second, continuously improve the standards for making the process better and better; finally, ensure that employees have sufficient knowledge and know how to apply the knowledge to achieve constant improvement. This is the process of innovation. These three steps repeat themselves in endless cycles. During this process, every ordinary employee has to think like a manager whose most important task is to make each employee understand and apply the philosophy of thinking.

But a key question is: How can we make our employees fully devoted themselves to contributing their best? In this regard, Tata Steel has a good practice experience.

We have a factory where workers have their own targets. In the first year, we told the workers, "How about we increase the target output by 20%?" The goal was realized. In the second year, we said, "How about we increase the target output by another 50%?" The result was also realized. It is unbelievable that our target has multiplied without new capital investment. I believe that there is still room for improvement in the future.

If we compare the 40,000-odd employees in Tata Steel to arrows, we can achieve amazing results when pointing 40,000 arrows at the same target. At Tata Steel, what we do is to encourage everyone to share their vision and aspire them to think.

Encourage the front-line staff to share the vision. If the implementation of vision is top-down after the board of directors defines the vision, it will be quite difficult to share vision among employees. I strongly believe that vision cannot be instilled through top-down rules. We should not try to get people to understand the vision through words. That's why we use the vision architecture rather than a simple statement to implement vision. The vision architecture allows everyone in the company to know their roles and contributions to the vision.

In December 2001, we held a two-day seminar with the topic of vision. Fifty senior executives participated in the seminar at which we have developed a vision blueprint for Tata Steel in the next 5 to 10 years, that is, what kind of company Tata Steel wants to be. Regarding this question, the management provided a lot of ideas and suggestions, and summarized them into five to six recommendations on the internal network. After that, I wrote a letter to more than 40,000 employees within the organization, asking them to express their opinions on these suggestions.

To our surprise, we received more than 8,000 responses from different levels of the company, of which 4,000 were from ordinary front-line employees. In this way, employees who are not well-educated can participate in the company's high-level discussion on strategy and vision.

Next we set up a team who had spent three or four months specializing in employees' feedback. Finally, in May 2002, we launched the vision of Tata Steel. The entire process of vision development allows employees to feel that this is not force-fed from the company's top executives, but the result of everyone's participation that represents their "own" expectations.

With such a consensus, the introduction and implementation of the vision has become smooth. According to the original plan, it would take five years to achieve the vision, but in fact it only took two years.

"Knowledge Journey." There is a knowledge management operation system within Tata Steel. Instead of only being set up for senior managers, the system requires the participation of every employee. Every month or two, different departments will call together 40 to 50 employees to be involved with a project named "Knowledge Journey". Usually, the project asks members to discuss around a topic in about 3 hours. Topics can be very specific, such as solving the problem of machine oil leakage. Employees from different departments but relevant to the specific topic will express their opinions. Through the discussion of these very petty issues, Tata Steel has formed a common way to solve the problem, which also contributes to the continuous improvement of the aforementioned operational processes. Also, the project provides an opportunity for each employee to consider problems at a certain ideological level. Participating in such projects can motivate employees. Today, continuous improvement has become the DNA of Tata Steel by deeply integrating into the company's operations and management.

In addition, we have a mentor system in which each senior manager is assigned to building up a connection with three employees. I was also assigned to three employees. I often interacted with them and invited them to my house for dinner. Such a system is a good way to share values in an organization.

Of course, this does not mean that we do not have dark moments, such as redundancies. We also have to reduce the staff, but attempt to do it in a more humane and gentle way, which is quite different from many other companies. My son applied for a position in a leading Indian IT company and finally got an offer letter. However, he has not received a call from this company since then. When I met the CEO of the company at a conference, I told him about my son's experience. In Tata Steel's history, we have never treated any employee in similar way, whether in good or bad times. This is what I call "being truly genuine" rather than showing the so-called genuineness for others.

At Tata Steel, we have a sense of urgency and tolerance for failure. We emphasize the wisdom and value of our employees. I had interviewed five or six candidates who applied to the internal position to manage Tata Steel. I only asked them one simple question: Who is the greatest Indian person in the 20th century? The answers I got might surprise you — Bollywood star Amitabh Bachchan, cricket player Sachin Tendulkar.... Finally, I hired the girl who answered "Gandhi."

I Don't Like the Word "Acquisition"

Tata Steel's growth strategy is driven by the mission of "creating value for all the stakeholders". So we are not globalizing for the sake of globalization.

In this sense, Tata Steel's acquisition of Corus Steel in the UK in 2006 was not a whim, but a part of the company's strategy launched in 2002: Performing strongly in India, seeking more opportunities globally. This acquisition is an important milestone.

Tata Steel's acquisition philosophy is different from many those of other firms. First of all, I personally don't like the word "acquisition" because it can't accurately express our business concept. We will not conduct hostile takeovers unless the other side is willing to develop with us. In this sense, terms such as "cooperation" and "common development" are more suitable for us. Corus came to us in the beginning. Other steel companies from various places like Singapore and Thailand also came to us.

After the acquisition, we will not change the management of the other side, nor will we send Indian employees to the company. Instead, we rely more on the management of the original company to give them enough trust, because we believe that different operating entities have their own strengths and weaknesses, making it important for both companies to complement each other in their allocation of resources. Instead of being the master of the new company, we'd like to contribute our own advantages and achieve joint development with the other side through close cooperation.

Conflicts cannot be avoided in mergers and acquisitions (M&A), and cultural integration is the most important factor that might lead to conflicts. The most critical issue in M&A is how to be more patient and humane to fully demonstrate trust in the other side. For example, Western companies usually set goals and know in advance how to achieve goals before they set off. The ideological concept of Indian companies is: If you know how to get there, you would have already arrived. The habit of Indian companies is to set goals first without exactly knowing how to achieve them. Usually they know 30% or 50% of the answer to achieve the goals, and get the rest of the answer through trial-and-error. This is the biggest difference I have seen between emerging market companies and Western companies. Cultural difference plays a great role in solving this problem. In the West, due to the clear goal, employee compensation, executive compensation, and bonuses all depend on whether you meet your goals or exceed them. This ideological concept will directly affect business operations, which I think is the biggest difference.

On the other hand, even though we have global ambitions, we are still rooted in India. Our eyes have never left India and will not in the future. For us, India is still the most attractive country for steel manufacturing.

Against the Storm, Look to the Future

The steel industry is facing the challenge of attracting and retaining the "necessary talent", no matter in India or other countries. Please note that what I am talking about here is "necessary talents" rather than "top talents". The manufacturing companies are faced with the challenge that it is becoming increasingly difficult to attract talents compared with those industries that offer higher wages and a more relaxing work environment. To some extent, I am quite worried to see that many engineers and technical experts today reject the professional challenges posed by manufacturing companies, but are more and more fascinated by glamorous documentary research that lacks professional challenges.

Another key challenge for Tata Steel is manufacturing and mining technologies, especially the technologies related to protecting resources and the environment. Gaining enough iron ores and coal resources in the short and long term is another important factor in determining our future competitive position.

For the current economic slowdown, my concern does not lie in its short-term impact on the steel industry, but a more sustainable negative impact on us since the economic slowdown will reduce investment in upstream industries, such as iron ore and coal mines.

The current economic crisis is global and every company will be affected. Currently Tata Steel takes two steps to deal with the crisis. The first step is to "resist the storm." We have firstly measured the impact of the current economic distress by conducting in-depth research in different countries. In Europe, we consider closing some production lines after 6 months to 1 year to further reduce operating costs. On the other hand, we will speed up the continuous improvement of operations, cut the daily administrative and operating costs, with the aim of saving 1 billion pounds throughout the year. We are doing the same work in India, hoping to reduce the cost of 300 million dollars through the year.

Our second step is to "look to the future." After the economic crisis came to an end, we needed to quickly resume the pace of development to ensure a recovered company in the near future, such as a better adjustment of internal structure, the growth of productivity, proper retention of various production lines and factories after a thorough research. We have started to do such work since December 2008. Our current results are quite satisfactory.

Long-lived businesses have always endured great hardships. There are many long-life companies like Tata Steel in the world. Some have a life span of one hundred or two hundred years, and some Japanese companies even have a history of thousands of years. I believe that there are four key issues with regards to the secrets of the long-lived companies.

- *To be a part of the society.* Long-lived enterprises, whether in Japan, the United States, India or Europe, are all coexisting with society. Their development course must be deeply integrated into the development of society.
- *Adaptability.* It is the ability of a company to adapt to the environment. Change is everywhere, and companies must learn to adapt changes, in terms of the goals, systems, values, and visions.

- *Decentralization.* Power cannot be concentrated in the hands of one person, which is also the embodiment of leadership.
- *Financial Soundness.* The long-lived companies across the world are financially sound without many debts. Profitability can bring sustained growth. These companies always look to the long-term future instead of only the next several quarters.

Tata Steel is a very open company that provides equal opportunities to every employee. When I joined Tata Steel in 1966, I was just an ordinary trainee, but today I have become the CEO of this company. Everyone can realize their dreams in Tata Steel whose cultural environment values fast growth and transparency. My experience tells a story about a professional's growth in a company. This is an unforgettable journey that allows me to have full freedom to realize my dreams and learn to respect others. If there is an afterlife, I am still willing to work for Tata Steel rather than those trendy IT companies.

About the Author

B. Muthuraman is General Manager and CEO of Tata Steel. He joined Tata Steel as an ordinary trainee in 1966. Through 30 years of accumulating experience in the Iron and Steel and Engineering Development Departments and Marketing Departments, he became the general manager of Tata Steel in 2001 after successfully leading the famous cold-rolled steel coil project in record time. He said that his own experience proves the fairness and greatness of this company. This article was originally published in the 8th issue of *CEIBS Business Review* in 2009.

XI

Wang Shi Hovered Between the Eastern and Western Cultures

Zhu Qiong

Unexpectedly, one hour after interviewing Wang Shi, I received another call from him, "You mentioned Laurence Sterne's *Tristram Shandy* in the interview, and I need to explain that I have not read it yet." This question was written in the interview outline, but I did not get the chance to ask it.

It seems that two and a half hours is not enough to interview Wang Shi. Throughout the interview, Wang Shi has been trying to lead our way of thinking with his ideas. However, after leading Vanke for more than 20 years, this "enterprise godfather" with a strong sense of control has fallen into serious bewilderment due to various uncertainties about the future.

Wang Shi confides his uneasiness in his new work *A Soul is Hovering*, "As an entrepreneur, the homework I must do is to understand the laws of the market and explore the future of the enterprise. The more homework I do, the more I realize that there is a need to rethink some of the simplest and basic questions about the value of life and business to explore the source of the spirit and the essence of reason. Can we be close to the truth and the answer through all the efforts? I have no idea."

In the era of pursuing scale and speed, Wang Shi once had great ambition. In his book *Roads and Dreams* for commemorating the 20th anniversary of

Vanke, Wang Shi's subtext is that "Vanke will enter the world's top 500 enterprises sooner or later." However, when Vanke achieved a leapfrog sales growth from 2 billion yuan to 10 billion yuan, Wang Shi realized that "we have run so fast that our soul can't keep up." Does the future development have to be spiraling? Wang Shi shook his head slightly, and said, "This is just your assumption." In his view, uncertainty also indicates contingency and absurdity. Therefore, "we may move toward to higher levels, or to lower levels in the future. Will our journey surely go to the higher levels? It is not certain."

"I may leave the world 30 years later, but where will the company go? What will support Chinese companies for the long-term growth?" Wang Shi asked.

Deal with Impetuosity and Rationality

In the Chinese market, Wang Shi and Vanke, which he founded, have always shown an "unorthodox" image to the public. He gives up the idea of being a boss, says no to bribery, proposes a "turning point theory", establishes a professional manager system, creates a culture that releases individuality and respects people, and insists on the concept of "rejecting the profit of more than 25%". Moreover, in the real estate industry, he also takes the lead in proposing the strategy of housing industrialization and a green residential vision in accordance with the concepts of environmental protection and energy conservation.

These "unorthodox" behaviors have been spoken highly of by many entrepreneurs. Ning Gaoning, the chairman of COFCO Group, regarded Wang Shi's specialization strategy as an important act in the history of Chinese enterprises development. Ning Gaoning has engaged in diversified operations, both in his previous company China Resources Group and the COFCO Group. Therefore, he knows how much courage it takes to return to specialization from diversification, as "the conceptual, structural, and financial impacts will make people irresolute". But Wang Shi persisted to the end. And the company maintained steady development in the process. Ning Gaoning believes that this reflects Wang Shi's strong belief and will to change himself.

We originally thought that Wang Shi would be proud of his uniqueness. However, he just replied with an understatement, "This is the result of continuous trial and error with the attempt to correct errors according to the laws. For example, the reason to choose specialization strategy is the unsuccessful experiences of diversification. We have always been true to some things originally thought during the process of trial and error."

Wang Shi said that his habit of rational reflection was influenced by Western culture. "We do not advocate reflective thinking in our traditional Chinese culture." He undisguisedly admitted his identity of being a scientific instrumentalist of Western rationality. He described the process of establishing Vanke as a process of copying the Western model.

The pursuit of Western culture began early in Wang Shi's youth time. He experienced the "Cultural Revolution" in eighth grade. At that time, Balzac, Dickens, Tolstoy, Pushkin filled his heart in place of Chinese classical cultural works. His engagement in sports such as mountain climbing, hang gliding, and rowing race, as well as his pursuit of human liberation and individual release, all reflect the ideals and rationality of Western values.

Schumpeter said, "There is one group of entrepreneurs who has the will to conquer and the energy to fight. The pursuit of success is not to get the result of success, but to achieve success itself." Wang Shi quite agrees with this statement. When he went to Shenzhen to find his own way in the world at the age of 32, he was in the pursuit of realizing his individual value. Therefore, his motivation to establish a business is very different from those who want to own a family business. It is this difference that urged him to give up the idea of being a boss, and create Vanke that provides equal opportunities and values people's capabilities rather than their backgrounds.

The concept of not being a boss lays the premise and foundation for the professional and commercial management of Vanke. Since he is not the boss, under his leadership Vanke has lost the motivation to pursue an exorbitant profit. Without the driver of exorbitant profit, Vanke is more likely to use strategy to determine business choices and resist temptations. Without the desire for exorbitant profit, Wang Shi and other professional managers in Vanke can hold the bottom line of refusing bribery.

Wang Shi said with a smile, "Vanke and I sitting steadily in the volatile real estate industry has something to do with the implementation of these rational business principles."

However, there is a premise of all these rational business principles, that is, a standardized and market-oriented business environment. But China's real estate market has a distance from realizing this premise, which can demonstrate Wang Shi's advancing ideas and behaviors. Wang Shi is the only representative from enterprises among the eight "Practitioner Benchmarks of Chinese Dream" selected by *Southern Weekly* in 2009. Wang Shi chose "no bribery" as his benchmark. Speaking of this matter, Wang Shi jeered, "I don't think that 'no bribery' should be the bottom line of the business, but it has gone so far as to become a benchmark. Who is to blame? Me? *Southern Weekly*? Or the society? It is self-evident." Wang Shi began to propagate "no bribery" as early as a few years ago, and recently he seldom mentioned it. And he brings it up again in this selection event for two reasons. First, "I thought everyone had recognized 'no bribery', but this event made me realize that many people were not aware of its importance, so I have to bring the term up again as it is the future trend." Second, "I mainly said it to the Vanke people to prevent them slackening to make an exception in their favour. That would be a terrible thing." Vanke now has 20,000 people from 32 cities. "As long as someone pays the bribes in Vanke, it is my problem." The absolute words from Wang Shi show his determination to hold the bottom line. There was a time that one of Wang Shi's subordinates wanted to play around in the gray area to make a big order, and even flew to Wang Shi's office in the company base. He choked out through tears, "Can you do me a favor? Only once. I can beg you on my knees." Wang Shi said, "You don't need to kneel to me. No is no." At last, the subordinate had no choice but to leave with hatred.

If "no bribery" only leads to the loss of some orders for Vanke, the controversy caused by the "turning point theory" proposed by Wang Shi has pushed him and Vanke to the opposite side of the industry. Although Wang Shi has always insisted that "turning point theory" is a rational judgment based on market changes, his peers believe that it is Vanke's approach to suppress competitors to occupy the market.

There are other things that make Wang Shi unable to be at ease. Wang Shi talks about the "Donation Affairs" in 2008 every time he meets the media. "What is the difference between my statements and those of multinational companies? What is the difference between Vanke's performance to relieve disaster and that of multinational companies? However, when consumers smashed and vandalized Carrefour and KFC, Ministry of Commerce stood up and spoke for them, but no one spoke for Vanke!" Here, the "big" person revealed his true emotions in front of the public like common people. He is a person who quite cherishes his reputation, and is reluctant to be misunderstood by the public.

Judge and Weigh Properly to Handle Conflicts

Never regard Wang Shi's unconditional apology for the "Donation Affairs" and his subsequent complaints as inconsistency. In fact, this is his method of handling conflicts. The previous apology was to subside the negative comments on Vanke from the outside world, and the subsequent complaint was to preserve the rational image of conducting himself.

Wang Shi's persistent pursuit of dreams, expression of his individuality, and unwillingness to follow the trend when conducting himself and doing business will inevitably bring lots of conflicts between Vanke, himself and the outside world. Therefore, the skill of judging and weighing properly is essential for him to live a wonderful life. When it comes to judging and weighing, Wang Shi smugly moved to the sofa to sit comfortably. "Entrepreneurs who walk too fast might become martyrs; otherwise they will become followers. So, this is a process of judging and weighing to advance, with a premise of holding true to the ideal and kind wishes."

In fact, Wang Shi's choice of reputation over profit is the result of judging and weighing. His personality makes it impossible for him to refuse reputation. But in the Chinese culture of "shooting the bird which takes the lead", he can only keep his reputation when staying far away from the interests so that others have nothing on him.

Wang Shi also shows strong ability of judging and weighing in defining and promoting business strategies. Vanke's strategy of residential housing industrialization has aroused doubts and criticisms from thc outside world. Some say it does not suit the Chinese market, while others believe Wang Shi is experimenting with the money of shareholders. Despite many disputes, Wang Shi still decided to make 2014 the deadline of realizing this strategy. However, he shows skills of judging and weighing in terms of the shareholder interests and strategic input. To avoid shareholders' loss, Vanke has made gradual input to ensure that the development area of residential housing industrialization only accounts for 13 percent of the total development area so as to evenly distribute the added cost into the traditionally developed products.

Wang Shi also wants to utilize external resources. Thus, he publicizes housing industrialization in various events. "One reason is to get the attention and supports from the government," Wang Shi said with a sly smile. In fact, someone has already been willing to pay the bill. He revealed, "Housing industrialization gives Vanke strong bargaining power in buying land."

Green housing is a further strategy of housing industrialization. Wang Shi wants more recognition and support for this strategy from the government, consumers and shareholders. Therefore, Vanke spent heavily on building the Vanke Ecology Museum at the Shanghai World Expo. We have heard the stories of this museum many times on different occasions, but this time, Wang Shi still patiently started their stories from the first one, the Golden Monkey. Why does Wang Shi work diligently on spreading green ideas?

"To tell the truth, Vanke does not do this to demonstrate its noble intention. Green housing is Vanke's differentiated business plan and philosophy, which is difficult for ordinary developers to achieve. If the government adds such restrictions on bidding, how can our competitors survive?" Speaking of this, Wang Shi was so excited that he leaned forward. Then he restrained himself, "Vanke's current brand is still at the level of good property management and respected corporate. This is not enough. We want our brand to be recognized as Starbucks by consumers. We want to lead people's green lifestyle."

However, this depends to a large extent on the strategy based on the legal regulations made by the government. Wang Shi cannot guarantee whether he can finally succeed. "This is Vanke's philosophy. We have no choice but to propose the idea to the government."

In addition to the strategy, Wang Shi believes that business operation is another issue that requires leaders to judge and weigh. "For example, we need to judge and weigh efficiency and democracy within the company." People who joined Vanke from the outside, especially those from private companies and foreign companies, initially find it hard to adapt to Vanke's steady work pace. One has to talk himself hoarse to persuade the relevant party to push an issue. Once, a directly assigned executive even rushed to seek help from Vanke's general manager Yu Liang, but Yu could not help him by giving an order for enforcement. The reason is that Vanke advocates absolute respect for people, and order enforcement is based on the premise of fully understanding the other side.

Even Wang Shi himself has encountered resistance to enforcement. In 2006, Wang Shi proposed to achieve 100% fine decorated houses in 3 years, which caused objections from some first-line managers. At that time, Vanke's proportion of fine decorated houses was 30%, exceeding the average level in domestic real estate industry by 12% to 13%. The reason for managers' conflict is that the roughcast houses were also in short supply and quite profitable at that time. But when it comes to the fine decorated houses, it is not only difficult to guarantee the quality, but will extend the delivery date by at least three months. The delay will immediately affect the profits and returns of the executors. "Refuse easy money, but go looking for trouble!" Of course the first-line managers could not figure it out. However, the reason they officially gave to resist fine decorated houses is that "consumers do not accept decorated houses".

Although Wang Shi understands their real reasons for resistance, he did not expose it, nor did he enforce the order. Instead, he communicated with them following on the given reason. "Consumers are laymen of housing decoration, but we are experts. So what is going wrong when things completed by experts cannot be accepted by consumers?" Then, Wang Shi explained why he proposed this plan, "For the housing industrialization, the roughcast house is only a semi-finished product. How can we achieve housing industrialization if we can't even decorate the house? In addition, to dispel the misgivings of the executives, Vanke also adjusted the assessment indicators for the first-line managers. After three years, Vanke's fine decorated houses accounted for 85% in 2009. Wang Shi still accepted the figure though it did not reach 100%, showing his skill of judging and weighing. He set the 2010 target at 95% in 2010.

Because the real estate industry is relatively extensive and profitable, Vanke's efficiency has brought few negative impacts. Wang Shi frankly said, "Vanke has become what it is today without special fine operation or great management. This market is very extensive, and a little bit more efforts will give you returns and recognition by the market."

However, the era of extensive operation cannot last forever. Vanke's efficiency for enforcement cannot be ignored, which is rooted in Vanke's culture of absolute democracy. Therefore, Vanke needs to add new content to business culture when moving forward. But what to add? "I don't know yet." Wang Shi answered after some time of thinking.

An Uncertain Future

Wang Shi has always studiously avoided Chinese culture in the process of establishing Vanke. "I admit that I have limited knowledge in Chinese culture. Because the society was excluding traditional Chinese culture when I was accepting education. Therefore, my understanding in this field is quite shallow." So, the complete copy of the Western modern enterprise system has become his shortcut. "However, until now, my understanding of the Western systems has only remained at a stage of knowing how without knowing why," Wang Shi said very frankly. But when Vanke needs to add new cultural connotations in the next stage of development, or finds it inevitable to have conflicts in integrating Chinese and Western cultures, "Things that I originally avoided or was confused cannot be avoided now, and I must face and explore them." So he re-took the route of Buddhist Xuanzang to worship Jerusalem, look at the cathedral with reverence, ask questions about the Judaism and Christianity to explore the evolution of Western corporate systems, the relationship between Eastern and Western cultures, and the elements that can combine the two cultures so as to "know why".

However, going to the root of the Western and Eastern culture is as difficult as getting the scripture from the Western Heaven. Although Wang Shi has made great efforts, he still has many doubts. He sighed with emotion, "It seems impossible for my generation of leaders in Vanke to make foreign things serve China and integrate Eastern culture and Western culture. Can it be achieved in the future? That is the business of the new generation of leaders."

For Vanke's future, some employees hold the view that "Wang Shi's authority in Vanke is irreplaceable. The existence of Wang Shi makes Vanke's management relatively simple. If Wang Shi leaves, the company will become quite complicated." Hearing this, Wang Shi was silent for a moment, and said with a smile, "There is no way to prove this statement now. We need to wait until I leave. But it is only one of the possibilities."

For Vanke, a company which is founded with his own hands but does not belong to him, Wang Shi used to hold an easy and free attitude. "When I am no longer the chairman of the board, you can do whatever you want. That is none of my business." However, he seems to be a little more concerned recently, "If Vanke gives up residential housing one day, I will raise my hands to express opposition even after death."

Wang Shi originally planned to leave Vanke at the age of 58, and he is 58 years old this year. "The fact that I have not left Vanke proves that I still have values as a chairman. I seem to play all day, but I still play the role of the leadership in the ideological level," Wang Shi said carefully while staring at the sofa. Suddenly, he switched the conversation, joking, "I have no room for retreat. I have spoken to the outside world that I am willing to play a bigger role on a larger stage, such as the CEO in a large state-owned enterprise." Suddenly he made a face like he had been wronged, and said, "But the State-owned Assets Supervision and Administration Commission of the State Council (SASAC) does not extend an olive branch to me."

It is hard to imagine that Wang Shi, a straightforward person who pursues freedom will yearn to be a CEO in a large state-owned enterprise, a role that requires "dancing with shackles". Maybe he is just joking. But we can imagine that Wang Shi's life energy has not been fully released in Vanke. He climbed before 60 years old, and sailed before 70 years old, experiencing a rich life in addition to his career.

So far, both Wang Shi and his Vanke can be considered successful. However, Wang Shi has such a question: "Does success mean greatness?" He believes that success might be achieved by accident. Therefore, "the past performance is unexpected, and the future is also uncertain."

Lots of uncertainties made Wang Shi bewildered. Fortunately, he has a clear goal of living a "healthy and abundant life". Therefore, at the end of the interview, he rushed back to Shenzhen to travel around Taiwan by bike the next day. And he just participated in the China Sailing Cup the day before our interview.

Attached: Wang Shi's Words

Rejecting the Profit of More Than 25%

It is a basic principle of economics that prices fluctuate round the value according to demand. The price may be lower than the value when there is more supply, and it will go up when in short supply. But it will eventually fluctuate round the value. When an industry is highly profitable, everyone will enter it, leading to a decreasing profit. Except monopoly industries, which industry will continue to have high profits?

Vanke is doing business according to this simple principle. But everyone is pursuing opportunism in China because they can't resist its temptation.

Vanke can grasp this simple truth, which reflects the company's cultural dimension. The cultural dimension requires us to grasp the truth.

About "Copying"

Subjectively, Vanke has copied the Western modern enterprise system without combining the Western and Eastern culture. We hold an open attitude to absorb foreign things. We are supposed to remain and combine local culture in the process of abortion. But I fully copy it without making combination. I admit that I have limited understanding of Chinese culture. I have to firstly figure out what "Chinese culture" is. How can I make use of it before knowing it? So I choose the mode of complete copy.

Modern enterprise is the product of Western Christian civilization, which becomes the mainstream in the world and has the right to say. It will be a problem if you utilize it before learning it well. Is it an extreme saying? Yes, it is. Is it proper? Not really. But at least it is feasible for Vanke, so I will not be confused on this point.

There is a big difference between the Eastern culture and the Western culture. The Eastern culture believes man's nature is good at birth. But not all of them are good people. There are also bad guys. Who should we use? Of course we must make use of good people and fight against the bad people. This results in many interesting phenomena, such as recommending the capable based on favoritism. This is not the case in the Western culture, which proposes that we are all sinners in front of God. According to the Western culture, man's nature is evil at birth, but they all have a good side. So the Western culture encourages people to play to their good side and constrain people through regulative systems. The current corporate system is based on this thought. It assumes that all people make mistakes, so regulation is a must to constrain them.

According to Chinese tradition, people do not restrict themselves but tend to restrict others. Vanke's system restricts both others and ourselves. Although the company has gone a long way through continuous trial and error, there are not major problems in Vanke thanks to our corporate culture.

About Integration

Doing business requires asking questions. In 2007, Vanke became the world's largest housing development company. In the future, all of the top 10 housing development companies will come from China. Therefore, in some sense, we must undertake ethical responsibilities. At this time, we can no longer stay in the phase of "just knowing it". We have to understand many things that were originally avoided or confusing.

The book *A Soul is Hovering* aims to "know why". The modern enterprise system and Western civilization are the products of Christian Civilization. Christianity is closely related to Judaism. You have to know what it is before understanding how it has evolved.

So what about the future? Dealing with the issue of the true integration between Eastern culture and Western culture is unavoidable. I used to avoid learning Chinese culture, but then I found that it cannot be ignored.

About the Author

Zhu Qiong is a former senior reporter of the *CEIBS Business Review*.
This article was originally published in the 12th issue of the *CEIBS Business Review* in 2009.

XII

Zhang Chaoyang: Through the Flames

Liu Zhengzheng

> "In fact, every idea is a flame. You will be burned if you only stare at these thoughts. But if you throw yourself into the fire and run through the flames, you will not be burned."

Charles Zhang, the famous Zhang Chaoyang, has been online in Sohu Weibo all day recently. Soon after we sat down, he suddenly saw the news that Zhou Libo had become a user of Sohu Weibo, and found it did not appear on the front page. He immediately raised his head to tell his subordinate, "Call XXX to deal with the issue now." For a moment, I seemed to see another two crazy people in the area of product experience, Ma Huateng and Zhou Hongyi (forgive me for saying this since these two people just had fought a business battle).

Then he could hardly sit still. The fierce competition in Weibo is a matter of life and death. The survival requires serious considerations. In this regard, he used a lot of military words, "Wars are going on in the United States every day." "Don't be afraid of war. Only wars limited by certain rules can promote the progress of the entire Internet." "Move forward, or you'll fall behind. There is no intermediate zone. It is all or nothing." His goal seems not so high, "We will win the war when Sohu Weibo reaches a market share close to Sina Weibo."

In the past five years, Sohu has been moving towards the goal of "one-stop service provider" with its competitors Baidu and Tencent. In all fairness, although Sohu's performance is not as promising as that of his two peers, the company still has some gains. Today Sogou owns the largest keyboard input software in China, making it occupy the lower right corner of computer desktop of Chinese people together with QQ and 360; and its subsidiary game company Changyou that was successfully listed on Nasdaq has brought steady cash flow for Sohu.

At the same time, Charles is also thinking about the ultimate proposition of life. In 2008, in his blog post titled *Basic Contradiction in Life*, the doctor of physical science graduating from MIT pointed out the basic contradiction between "efficiency" and "wisdom", arguing that "the pursuit of efficiency is the root of anxiety, as well as the enemy of wisdom and relief". He also clearly gives the solution: "Anxiety is the result of thought, and carefreeness is the result of not thinking."

Charles bought a luxury yacht and relaxed on the shipboard that he could swing gently in the sun in Hainan province. For many ordinary people who are still busy in making a living, Charles' behavior after some thoughts may seem slightly queer. It is actually not a big deal. A small yacht, in the eyes of a person who holds a philosophy of "I do not care", is only an attitude to living in the present.

Individuals are to the company as the soul is to the body. They are always intertwined. Charles tried to separate himself to forget the surroundings and even themselves. He told me, "Being choosy and moderate in eating, plus doing yoga and exercise will make people in a very clean state." Also, "Sitting in meditation can produce psychological hints to solidify good things through repetitive motions."

But "the time goes like lightning." Facing the crowded and noisy Weibo platform like the search engine industry in previous years, Sohu fell behind again. Charles suddenly woke up and began to change himself, starting from his way of speaking. He said on Weibo, "I plan to stop talking in the way of standing on my dignity." He started to invite celebrities from all walks of life like a hospitable shopkeeper that never stopped talking. Otherwise, "financial security" and "vanity", the cornerstone of Blank Essence, will be threatened. He must defy death to defend them.

Web 2.0 is a big fire, and I hope that Charles will run through the raging flames, safe and sound.

People with "Plenty" are More Likely to be Enlightened

CEIBS Business Review (hereinafter referred to as CBR): You have disappeared from the public views for the past two years. What were you thinking?

Charles Zhang: I just want to have my own time and have a little more fun. However, it seems that I let go of Sohu while at the same time I am still in charge.

CBR: It's hard to imagine that a leader who has been engaged in the Internet industry for more than 10 years fails to recognize the cruelty of this industry.

Charles Zhang: Maybe my research on Silicon Valley may not be deep enough. Lacking sufficient attention and business acumen, I think it is enough with several capable people helping me since the separation of Changyou has brought great cash flows. But the Web 2.0 revolution has broken out so fast in China that it is impossible to fight by relying on one department or team. I did not realize that then.

CBR: "Anxiety is the result of thought, and carefreeness is the result of not thinking." Have you lived a life of "not thinking" during the last two years?

Charles Zhang: I am attempting to stop thinking, but the attempt itself requires me to think.

CBR: Will the war of Web 2.0 make you anxious?

Charles Zhang: Life is a fire array filled with all kinds of thoughts. You need to stare in one direction and run forward to rush through the fire. In fact, every idea is a flame. You will be burned if you only stare at these thoughts. But if you throw yourself into the fire and run through the flames, you will not be burned.

CBR: What are your new experiences and understandings of the basic contradiction between "efficiency" and "wisdom" that you proposed in 2008?

Charles Zhang: Many people have pains. They want to open their heart knots through work. This is wrong. Work is a type of intention, and any intention will cause anxiety. Intention means attention to the negative side, something that will enlarge its negative effects to lead to anxiety. The aim of throwing oneself into work is to reach an excited state, not to seek relief. When you work hard without trying to relieve yourself, you might get more relief.

CBR: How do you understand the words "Blank Essence" that you like?

Charles Zhang: Fundamentally speaking, it means that nothing truly matters. Financial insecurity, career insecurity, and the fear of being abandoned are all gone. Your life completely consists of interests. Eliminating such insecurities is a cautious process, which firstly requires you to have "Plenty". Successful people have lots of resources. People are more likely to achieve "Blank Essence" when these resources are very substantial and hard to be taken away. Many writers claim that one book can free people only to sell more copies. In fact, only people with Plenty are more likely to be enlightened.

CBR: Therefore, "Blank Essence" means the opposite of persistence. Then are you returning to the battlefield to show persistence?

Charles Zhang: People are more likely to obtain extrication and achieve "Blank Essence" with "Plenty". But the winner takes all in the Internet industry. The half-controlling state has impacted my "Plenty". After returning to the battlefield, I have gained a basic sense of security on the one hand. On the other hand, I have little desire to be a great entrepreneur, or to establish a long-lasting enterprise. Interest plays an important role in my return. I can play Weibo all day without feeling tired. Interest is a source of creativity. It is difficult for one to be creative when he/she have a strong sense of purpose.

I was Deceived by My Fame

CBR: You said on Weibo, "the biggest obstacle to our progress is ignorance and conceit." As the saying goes, "tens of millions of sailboats pass by the capsized ships, and thousands of trees flourish in front of the withered trees." Can you talk about your experiences about this?

Charles Zhang: As the first-generation Internet company in China, Sohu failed to grow to be the biggest one. There are many objective causes. Success needs luck, which can be achieved by accident. For example, Li Yanhong is luckier than me. When I was financing, the Internet just experienced explosive development in the US. And no one believed that people could do Internet in China. In 1996, some people threw some money to financiers who went to the US only out of a blind interest in China. This is how my first investors came. They believed in whatever Wall Street and the media said. In 1999, after Sohu and Tom rose, Li Yanhong also went to the US for financing. But what he got was "Smart Money". It was probably that his investors asked him to focus his mind on search engines. But for many years, my investors have kept asking me, "Where does my money go? How about my earnings?" I can blame others, complaining that I am not lucky, because I entered the industry too early as a person who cut a way through the underbrush. I was covered all over with cuts and bruises in this process, but my followers could walk quickly. There are many other objective causes, such as the struggle with the board of directors, the incomplete conditions...

But there are also subjective causes. I was almost the first person in China to do Internet, in a way of giving enormous publicity to it. I became a celebrity like Yang Zhiyuan in the United States, the synonyms for "pioneer" and "digital hero" of China's Internet digitization. These things went to my head, making me see myself as a great person. In this case, I believed that my thoughts were always right. This is my ignorance.

On the one hand, my board of directors pushed me to earn money, placing me under huge pressure and I became anxious. I resisted the pressure. But on the other hand, I did not take the initiative to follow the evolution of the Internet. One evolution is directory navigation of great need at that time when there was not much content on the Internet, which explained Yahoo's rise. In 2001 and 2002, anything could be seen on the Internet. People were no longer satisfied with navigation. They needed to enter a keyword to see the result they were looking for pop up immediately. When the Internet evolved in this direction, I continued to be the celebrity, lost in the delusion that I was the most advanced person without thinking about the changes happening on the Internet. Sohu missed the opportunity to introduce a search engine, which was caused by my ignorance.

Then Sohu had experienced successes and failures. At a certain stage, I began to seek enjoyment to relax myself. I still had psychological entanglements. I complained about the trauma in those years, making up my mind to be technically-driven by fully communicating with technicians and product personnel to listen to what they said. Full communication did have an effect, such as the birth of Sogou input method software, and successful online games. But they were restrictive and not extensive. Because my English is pretty good, I could know what happened in Silicon Valley by taking a glance at Facebook and Twitter. But I barely read the news. The main reason is that I got slack for being too famous and being considered too successful. Chinaren, the earliest social network in China, was screwed up in my hands. I wrote those words to reflect on myself.

CBR: Sohu has increased its technical investment since 2005. What do you think of the technology-driven transformation that does not go far enough?

Charles Zhang: Our team has created a strong corporate culture. But I have not really thrown myself into it. Even if I don't have to do programming, I should at least be a crazy user and fan of technology and products. But I am not. I still feel superior and powerful. In this situation, if my subordinates are very capable by continuously proposing what should be done, I might take his opinions seriously. The dangerous thing is the lack of such subordinates when the leader is not a crazy user and fan of technology and products, which can cloud his judgement. In fact, the priority for leaders is to have a deep understanding of the product.

CBR: In other words, in the eyes of many people, you take the initiative to attract the media's attention by skateboarding in front of Tiananmen Square, and becoming the embodiment of digital heroes and fashion people. But they are actually the results of the views from the outside world that were around you, making it hard for you to step back and think about something clearly.

Charles Zhang: Yes, or you can say that I was deceived by my own fame.

Reinvent Yourself

CBR: Sohu is a matrix structure with many branches. Some people compliment about your coordination ability. What do you think of this evaluation?

Charles Zhang: I have not done enough. To grasp the direction for the company, I must turn into a fanatic product user. Good executing capacity requires me to know my subordinates well enough to assign them jobs commensurate with their abilities, making it important to spend time with different subordinates in daily life. I do have a lot of experiences in this area, which can also be used in the second-time undertaking. The schedule of the daily meeting, and the people I meet will decide what aspects of the company will be strong. Sohu is now more emphasizing product and technology. In the past, Sohu's marketing was also relatively strong, because Wang Hao (Sohu Co-President and Chief Operating Officer) can help me with many things. In the aspect of capital, Yu Chuyuan (Sohu Co-President and Chief Financial Officer) is also very good. With them, I can concentrate so much time on one specific area.

CBR: What three factors would you choose in making use of personnel?

Charles Zhang: Communication, tacit understanding, and trust. The relationship between people is like a tree that keeps growing. Continuous communication means to water the tree constantly. I have a tender personality and treat all on an equal footing. In their words, I am a kind-hearted man. But this might also be a problem for me due to not being strict enough. Authority and power are two different things. You are the boss, and your subordinates reporting to you does not mean that you have influential power to him. Your influential power is reflected on his respect and trust in you, which requires your integrity, vision and communication.

CBR: You said that "the company that really makes a difference must be the one whose founder has led the company for a long way." What is the logic behind this?

Charles Zhang: From the perspective of competitiveness, the best choice is a wise founder who can lead the company to the future. The less good situation is when a founder with poor capabilities is replaced by the professional team who introduces some entrepreneurial mechanisms to make correct decisions. The worst circumstance is that the founder leads the company to perish due to his narrow opinion. As a major shareholder who has led the company for so many years, I often warn myself that the narrowness of my thoughts will limit the company's development.

It is difficult for people to change themselves, but I believe that people can do that. I am not a person who is too observant of conventional standards. I am no longer young but still single, which defies what is proper in China. I am also unbridled in life. I have played music, danced and gone mountain climbing very well. I believe that I can reinvent myself, and this time I can bring the company into a new area. In fact, Jobs also reinvented himself. In his early years, Jobs had a lot of innovations, but also caused many troubles. He had a very ill temper and yelled at others savagely. Finally, the company drove him away. Then, after reflection, he grew up creatively and matured. Eventually, he brought Apple to a new realm.

CBR: Jobs' reinvention has made him pay a great price.

Charles Zhang: Yes! He was driven away by the company, but I have been firmly in place. He experienced such a long mental journey that his physical health was affected. My mental journey was not that long, and my physical health is getting better and better. I am not paying a huge physical and mental cost by relying on a method of reflection and self-regulation. Though my price is not huge, I also pay the price of time.

CBR: Is there anyone that taught you something in this process?

Charles Zhang: No, it's all by myself though thinking and reading.

Continue to Get Crazy and Market Off the Beaten Path

CBR: There is a saying that Sohu has three treasures: "Boss, lawsuits, and soft advertisements." In the previous days, you have demonstrated a unique image through many unusual behaviors for the company's development. Now you are going to enter a new battle, what kind of new image is going to be presented?

Charles Zhang: Continue to get crazy and market off the beaten path in an all-around way. The most important thing is to launch products popular with netizens.

CBR: There are two first-class public relations talents in the Internet world. You and Mr. Zhou Hongyi. How do you evaluate Zhou's performance of media communication in the 3Q war?

Charles Zhang: Amazing.

CBR: Are there any other talent in the same league as Zhou in China?

Charles Zhang: No.

CBR: How about you?

Charles Zhang: I don't have the courage to contend with others. I don't like it. In my view, conflict has a psychological cost. It is hard for me to live a long life with conflicts (He *laughs*). I am not used to solving problems through conflicts. I am a tender person, though I admit that I have made many brilliant achievements in marketing.

CBR: You fought against pirates in those years for the enterprise development. It was also a right thing. An important reason for the good results was the government's attention and support. How about your judgment on the situation around you?

Charles Zhang: On the whole, I am sensitive to many things. I sang songs popular with post-80s in karaoke. I am able to quickly accept new things.

CBR: How to keep young at heart?

Charles Zhang: This has something to do with my stay in the United States, as well as my self-reflection and blank essence. Blank essence means no judgment, restrictions or fetters. In this way, people in their 40s do not have to look old and clumsy, talk in a shrewd and deep way, wear proper clothes, eat proper meals, or have proper friends. But in reality, many people in my 40s are like this. They shoulder a huge responsibility for supporting their families. I am not like this. I go to the crazy disco, sing the latest songs in karaoke. I don't have many restrictions of "how things should be done". I can accept many new things.

CBR: The word "vanity" from your mouth is kind of cool.

Charles Zhang: I am a frank person. As a physics-major graduate, I feel good when talking without disguise after thinking it all out. What I am pursuing is the truth, so I hate false pride the most.

CBR: Is the false pride same as hypocrisy?

Charles Zhang: Hypocrisy is an obvious deception. False pride is deceiving oneself. In fact, a person of false pride may not want to be hypocritical, but he often speaks and behaves in a hypocritical way due to his inner understanding problem that leads to the vanity, a psychological effect. But he might not be aware of his dishonesty. Nothing can be done to solve this kind of "dishonesty", since some people may have such a thing in his heart. But I can recognize it and then expose it cruelly.

"I Don't Care" are My Favorite Words

CBR: Why "plan to stop talking in the way of standing on my dignity"?

Charles Zhang: When you think that you are a very insightful person who can write a suggestive phrase to enlighten people, you will organize your language in a stilted way. However, Weibo is a platform for free chat. I don't want others to consider me as a scholar, or a thinker. I am just an ordinary person who talks like anyone else. It is a kind of attitude that "I don't care". It is actually my favorite words. I am supposed to share my real feelings and thoughts on my Weibo.

CBR: But it seems that Shaanxi people are not like this in our mind.

Charles Zhang: Shaanxi people also have the attitude of "I don't care". These words are similar to "OM MANI PADME HUM" in Buddhism. There are also some swearing words often used by Shaanxi people. They work off anger, and can be considered as a channel to achieve blank essence.

All the time the contradiction between "efficiency" and "intelligence" has impacted our growth. From a naive child to a qualified grown-up, education has put people into a frame made up of anxiety by continuing to tell them what is the right judgment. The process is filled with constant negation that causes anxiety, fear and phobias. "You should not do this" and "you should do that" led to the anxiety of our generation, making us false people, that is, "the second-hand people". Young people's rebellion such as smoking in adolescence is actually a confrontation against education. Most people can't jump out of the frame of education. As a result, each of us becomes a brick of society, making the building of society inherently efficient to achieve steady social progress. However, efficiency also brings suppression and pain for every brick. When you have Plenty, there is such a space to relax yourself to hold the attitude of "I don't care". In this state, swearing words really work off angers. In fact, life is an art, and we can have relief in a very subtle area.

CBR: Currently which version is your own art of living?

Charles Zhang: It's 2.0. If you find the convergence point of "efficiency" and "intelligence", you can hugely improve the efficiency, because the real thing is very touching. When you really reach the state of "I don't care", while add some indicators of human society, you will have explosive and strong propagation force.

CBR: Can China cultivate a great company?

Charles Zhang: It is easier to establish a great company and win respect in the United States. When I made a speech at Stanford University recently, some listeners asked me about my views on Steve Jobs' speech at Stanford University. I have watched a part of his speech, according to which, "You must firmly believe in your dreams. Belief makes it come true." But I think what he said can't be realized in China, or we can say that certain evil factors are needed to make it come true. It is hard to win respect and create a great business in China. In China's business environment, one has to sacrifice his character and be wronged to be the most successful entrepreneur. Therefore, entrepreneurs who have made great achievements in China often look sullen and unhappy.

CBR: If there is a great company in China, do you think it is yours?

Charles Zhang: The problem is that I never regard the establishment of a great company as my purpose. I don't care!

About the Author

Liu Zhengzheng is senior reporter of the *CEIBS Business Review*. This article was originally published in the 12th issue of the *CEIBS Business Review* in 2010.

XIII

Be a Genuine Craftsman: The Source of Happiness for an Advertising Godfather

Liu Zhengzheng

Some people make a lot of money, but they do not like what they do for a living; some people are doing what they like, but they cannot afford an apartment in the city or town. Which one do you belong to? We choose to do business, but what has this choice brought to us? Thousands of years ago, our ancestors hunted animals. Today we hunt money. Is there a difference? Is what you do really what you want?

When we turn our sight back to ourselves, the enterprise is actually in the category of idealism. Your single thought will bring the myriads of changes for business that presents various values. However, where will your thought fall?

Gao Jun, the founder of Mei Kao Creativity Consulting Company, has the experience of working as a farmer and teacher, and establishing ties. Starting his business with 50 yuan, he is known as the "godfather of the Chinese local advertising industry" 20 years later. The industry leader who likes Chinese-style clothes, enjoys thinking, and has little interest in expanding the scale of business and capital market has summed up his distinctive corporate view in the process of communicating with the journalist of *CEIBS Business Review*.

The Hardest Thing for People is to Maintain Honesty

CBR: In the Chinese advertising industry, you have put forward some original theories. What are your new ones in the past two years?

Gao Jun: I have lived an unusual life with huge ups and downs. Having done business for about 20 years, my awareness on material things has gradually faded. Now I am thinking more about issues like who are we, where are we from and where are we going. Without clarifying these problems, it might be difficult for you to get to the destination of spirit when facing the future.

In a sense, I kind of hate business that people use each other and fight for some very specific goals. I have less awareness on these things. Now I do business by following the luck.

I don't think that big business means success, just like the world's creatures are of different sizes, from viruses to whales. The most important thing is that they are all living in the right place. It is also true for enterprises. Being big and strong is a complete empty talk. It doesn't make sense. What's important is survival of the fittest.

CBR: So what is the result of your thinking about people?

Gao Jun: The most important thing for people is to deal with three relationships. First, human and nature. For the enterprise, it is the relationship between the enterprise and the market. Just like nature selects species, market selects enterprise. The second one is the relationship between man and man. Business is a kind of relationship between man and man, making it necessary to be people-oriented whatever we do. Any business out of touch with people will not go far, because it is divorced from noumenon.

These two relationships can be learned from schools and books. The most difficult one is the relationship between self and self. I often tell people that when you see something, it is because you want to see it. Doing business requires insight. How does it come from? In my views, the first quality is honesty. Only honesty knows what you want to see. You will see prejudice if you want to see it. The most difficult thing for people is to know themselves. Specifically, it is whether they can understand the way they view the world around them, consciously or unconsciously.

CBR: What are the challenges for people to know themselves?

Gao Jun: The challenge lies in people's dishonesty. Many people are naturally dishonest due to the specific interests. We have lived in an environment of interest since we were young, and the nature of animals is the desire to possess things. A person with 1 billion yuan can still be unsatisfied, if he compares himself with the people with 10 billion yuan. But an old farmer with 5,000 yuan might feel like the richest man in the world. What really matters is not how much money you have, but your attitude towards it.

CBR: Why does this have something to do with honesty?

Gao Jun: You need to ask yourself what you want. Don't let your desires exceed your ability, otherwise you will definitely feel pain. Honesty is fundamentally different from credibility. We always talk about credibility in daily life, but I think it is pointless. If anyone can successfully deceive you, it is essentially you deceiving yourself, and others just provide an inducement. We rarely say that we are deceiving ourselves. But as long as you have the idea of leaving things to chance, you are starting to deceive yourself.

Doing Business is a Craft

CBR: So it will be smoother to do business when figuring out the relationships among people.

Gao Jun: Doing business is not the nature of society. It is something developed later, just a way to seek benefits. Hunting animals in the ancient time and hunting money today have nothing to do with human nature.

CBR: Doing business provides one more way for companies to obtain material wealth, making socialized mass production a reality. Can it be achieved with previous methods?

Gao Jun: The company needs to grow day by day due to the competition. It is actually as terrible as a Huangpu River whose tide keeps rising without ebbing, but it exists in the world in a rational way. Ignoring the moral bottom line is a terrible thing. Just like how cancer cells never stop growing even though they are aware that they will die with their host. Everyone knows that there will be problems with continuously growing companies, but who has stopped? None of them will stop, which is very pathetic.

CBR: Is it a possible growth pattern that one person keeps awake in an irrational group?

Gao Jun: I am only doing the business I should do, and resolutely refuse things against my conscience, such as asking for a rebate. Sorry, I will not do it. You can find someone else. I know that I can make more money by doing such things, but what is the point of earning more money for me? You have insulted me by doing this. In the end, I don't know if you will do me any harm or I will do you any harm. But one thing is sure, both of us will harm your boss. To avoid harming your boss, you need to be purged, but why should I get involved? If you are an honest person who does business honestly, you will definitely be more popular, though it also means you have to give something up.

CBR: So what does the company mean to humans? What is the relationship between humans and business?

Gao Jun: People have to face two words in their lifetime — reading and working. The so-called "reading" means life-long learning for people. There are different levels for reading, including "reading books, reading things, and reading people". The highest level is "reading people". You will understand the world when you can read people. The word "working" means that people should find something to do. Just like deer need to graze, and tigers need to hunt, people must have something to do in their life.

I never consider myself as a businessman. I only see myself as a craftsman. The TV series called *The Walking Feather Duster* tells us what is "craft" and what is the thing to make a living. The thing to make a living is a typical business. Business can be taken away, but not the craft. Others can buy the products made by your craft, but not your craft itself. There are various kinds of crafts, such as tinkering with a pan, and Einstein's research. The essence of craft is to bring value to others.

CBR: What is the relationship between craft and yourself?

Gao Jun: I have a craft, which makes me happy. I can draw my own circles. Craft does no harm to others. It does not satisfy one's needs at the cost of others' interests.

The Concept of "Four Follows"

CBR: How have these thoughts specifically helped you to lead a company to achieve today's status with 50 yuan in the beginning?

Gao Jun: I have a view of "four follows". These thoughts are against business rules to a large extent, but they have helped me to return to the state of conducting myself rather than doing business.

The first is "follow the luck". Speaking of luck, people often think of relatives and friends, which is actually too narrow-minded. There is an old saying in China, "small achievements rely on friends, while great achievements rely on competitors." Without Bush, there would be no Obama. Without Coca–Cola, there would be no Pepsi. These stories tell us that what really helps you in the world is the adverse circumstances, not the favorable ones. The true value of luck lies in the "undesirable conditions". The key person who affects you in your life must be someone who has criticized you and irritated you, such as a strict father, a friend who has deceived you, and a very tough boss. Those who can withstand the blow and turn the difficulties into motivation are the most inclusive and intelligent people. They are also the ones who truly cherish the "luck" in their life.

There are two levels for a world-beater. One is to beat everyone, and the other is to have no enemy in the world. So we never go to court and get irritated due to competition. Employees are free to enter and leave our company. Some have entered and left four times. They come to our company today, and leave tomorrow, but I still treat them as newcomers the next time they want to come.

The second one is “follow heart”. The so-called “heart” is an idea, a wish. The reaction on one thing made by a person represents his heart. The key to “follow heart” is “a heart of joy”. People must have sustained enthusiasms for something to have long-term joys and live a happy life. You need to ask yourself repeatedly about what things can give you continuous joys. That is what you should do. Otherwise, you can only measure happiness according to the common standards, such as power and fortune.

CBR: “A heart of joy” is critical, but the key issue is how to find it?

Gao Jun: The most important thing is whether you are willing to look for it. Nine of ten people can find it if they want to. Nowadays people don’t even have the thought to look for it, mainly because they fail to realize that there is such a thing as “a heart of joy”. Therefore, everyone cares for status and money. Fame and fortune are just indicators without power of understanding.

“Follow heart” does not have much price to pay, otherwise it must be false. For instance, what are the three most important factors in determining life for human beings? Air, sunlight and water. We can have the most important thing in life for free, and they have nothing to do with ability.

CBR: What is the third “follow”?

Gao Jun: “Follow personality.” People will basically be happy if they can “follow luck” and “follow heart”, at least they will not bring trouble on themselves. “Follow personality” is to follow one’s innate quality, which is also very helpful for people. A horse will give birth to a horse, and a sheep will give birth to a sheep. A sheep can never become a horse. Therefore, making use of personnel relies on identifying talents rather than training them. Ding Junhui’s father is very great, because he has discovered the strength of his son, and surrendered his last resource to take his son to Beijing. Ding Junhui failed to get good grades in school, and I don't think he can have good performance at work.

"Cannikin law" seems to be the most boring theory. First of all, neither of people or enterprises are cannikin. The fundamental strategy of "follow personality" is to make the longest board longer. People need to consciously exert their own strengths and avoid their own weaknesses instead of trying to change their own weaknesses, which is very important for your sense of well-being. Some people receive teacher's comment that "you are good all over except your hot temper" from elementary school. He has tried to change it by reading a lot of books, participating in many courses to understand many things. On the day of his retirement, he gets another comment from the leader, "Man, you are good all over. If your temper is not that hot, you will be better!" Can he change it? He can't.

CBR: What is the last "follow"?

Gao Jun: The fourth one is to "follow change". There are two ways to achieve that. On the one hand, if you can "follow luck", "follow heart", and "follow personality", change will be no challenge for you. On the other hand, if you cannot do that, you can just let it go. Do not be pressured by things that you can't change. This goes back to "follow luck."

The Reflections of Confucianism, Taoism, and Buddhism

CBR: It can be seen that your concept of "four follows" are largely reflections of Confucianism, Taoism, and Buddhism.

Gao Jun: According to my understanding, Confucianism is to solve the problem of how to possess things and control desire, helping you to walk on the right path, do good things for everyone. Taoism is to solve the problem of how to deal with fear of loss by telling you that don't be afraid of loss, because "hows and whys" need to be constantly perfected. People don't have to follow certain rules. Just like the story of "Chuang Chou dreaming of a butterfly", one can escape from worldly society with detachment. Confucianism makes you more and more ambitious in a gradual way to help you constantly achieve bigger dreams. But sometimes it is hard to tell the difference between dream and desire. According to Taoism, do nothing and everything is done. One needs to think about why to do something at a certain point. It gives people relief when you encounter setbacks, when you lose, or when you can't live according to your ideal state. Buddhism makes you feel at ease, helping you to get rid of greed, hatred, or delusion to return to the moment and eternity in life, and you can grasp life by yourself. Why these three things exist in Chinese culture simultaneously and cannot be separated from each other is because they meet the complex needs of people at different levels.

CBR: Regarding the thoughts of Confucianism, Buddhism and Taoism, only Confucianism shows a positive attitude, and the other two are different from the business expansion in the market economy. Can Chinese traditional culture be in line with market economy?

Gao Jun: Where is the bonding point of market economy and traditional Chinese culture? I think it is "enough is as good as a feast". The market economy is not limited to the word "target". Which degree of doing cold tea business can be considered good? To open a consulting company is like to be a private adviser who needs to do what he should do. It is not one football game after another. We cannot see the result immediately, and the most important thing is the word "life".

About the Author

Liu Zhengzheng is a senior reporter of the *CEIBS Business Review*. This article was originally published in the 6th issue of *CEIBS Business Review* in 2010.

XIV

The Parent Zong Qinghou

Zhi Weiyong

While both of them are patriarchal leaders who take control and make decisions, and both started their businesses in 1987, Huang Guangyu and Zong Qinghou have different stories. While Huang who led GOME Group (GOME) fell from grace, Zong who led Hangzhou Wahaha Group (Wahaha) managed to stay standing. What are the rooted causes apart from the superficial reasons?

Paternalistic leadership is rarely seen, or even unthinkable in the contemporary West, because it is inextricably linked with dictatorship, bureaucracy, risk, and failure. This concept has also affected Chinese domestic companies, so people did not feel very shocked by Huang Guangyu's incident of ending up in prison.

In comparison, it is unexpected that Zong Qinghou has stood for more than 20 years and never fell down in the storms. How can he manage to do that?

Indeed, Zong Qinghou is a genius. His personal entrepreneurial talents make him a master with no teacher. He is able to manage a large company with 260,000 employees. Systematically speaking, he has achieved the "three leaderships" proposed by some scholars, which includes authoritative leadership, benevolent leadership, and moral leadership. From the following dialogue, we can see how he has acted on these three dimensions.

What deserves more of our attention is a value orientation revealed by him, that is, the relationship between "I" and the company.

There is no outside pressure for this interview, but Zong Qinghou does not change his previous view, "My daughter is not necessarily the successor." We have no idea of his inner thoughts, though we are convinced of the attitude of a business founder with "paternalistic leadership" to the inheritance of his family business. No matter forced or not, Zong Qinghou reveals a complex uncertain emotion, but he is certain about "as long as we can ensure that the successor is an able man".

Given this answer, can we come to the conclusion that Zong Qinghou places enterprise above himself and his family?

Similarly, there are some other sayings from Zong:

- "I created Wahaha by myself, but it eventually belongs to the society. I can only enjoy a little benefit, because Wahaha will ultimately create wealth for the country."
- "The purpose of starting business in the beginning is to improve my life quality, and now I have to consider increasing the living standards of my employees."
- "Now I have so many employees who need to make a living, and the government also wants a little more tax revenue from me every year. Meanwhile, the society also gives high expectation on us."
- "Now employees hope that I can work for a few more years for their benefits, so I am working for them."

These statements sound high-profile, and some negative reports about Wahaha have raised doubts, but we would rather believe that these words reflect the true value of Zong Qinghou. On the one hand, all the employees and dealers have stood firmly on the side of Zong Qinghou during the business battle with Danone. On the other hand, only by detaching "I" from "surroundings" and "others" can we distinguish the boundaries of "legal" and "illegal", "right" and "wrong". In this way, the risk of dictatorship and human greed might be eliminated in the process of "maximizing corporate value".

In fact, apart from Huang Guangyu and Zong Qinghou, a number of local enterprises have achieved success under the paternalistic leadership of "heroic style". But, one day, enterprises will no longer belong to "parents". What will their future be?

CBR: People often say that leadership is an art. What do you think of this view?

Zong Qinghou: Leadership is indeed an art. There are particular skills for leaders to reach their goal, and to motivate the subordinates to do things happily according to his own purposes. During this process, the leader needs to combine the incentive system with the competition system. Wahaha implements a system in which leading cadres take up a job through competition every year, from the heads of various departments to the general managers of each company. So whether the leading cadres can go to their posts or not is dependent on the employees' evaluation. This year, about five or six people are removed from their leadership positions, and they all assent cordially to the decision. Since there is a big gap between the compensation of heads and deputy heads of departments, the deputy heads have an incentive to strive to be the head. Competition and struggle are two things. Without a competitive mechanism, there is no driving force for development.

Both compensation incentives and vision incentives are important. In terms of compensation incentives, Wahaha implements the Employee Stock Ownership, giving annual bonus for each employee. By doing this, everyone's income is tied to the enterprise development level. As for the vision incentives, Wahaha attempts to make employees feel that their jobs have a promising future and that they enjoy a high position in society. The employees will have a sense of honor and work hard when the company has good scale and reputation, and provides a promising welfare system.

Moreover, companies have different incentive goals at various development stages with employees of different qualities. In the early years after the company was founded, Wahaha was small in scale, and most employees were migrant workers. The main purpose then was to make money. Every week, I asked the staff to go out for dinner. My employees felt that their boss was very generous. Now things are different. Most of the employees are university graduates, and many of them even have Masters and Doctorate degrees. They have requirements for both material and spiritual rewards. Materially, in addition to Employee Stock Ownership, the company buys houses every year before selling them to employees at cheap prices, and builds low-rent housing for employees from other places. Spiritually, Wahaha proposes the slogan of striving to be a century-old store, aiming to enter the list of the world's top 500 business.

In general, the art of leadership is to combine your personal goals with your employees' goal, so that they are in awe of you, but do not hate you. It is difficult for companies to develop if leaders have no authority. However, in the process of establishing authority, you need to make your employees feel that you are reasonable and care for them. So they will believe that life will get better and better if they follow you.

CBR: Wahaha has not had a deputy general manager since its establishment, making you the only one at the decision-making level. Your management philosophies include "democratic centralism", and "(decentralizing) power on minor issues, while (centralizing) power on major issues". So what are the minor issues that can be decentralized, and the major issues which must be seized by your hands?

Zong Qinghou: There can only be one person in the company to make the final decision, just as there is only one party in power in China. For me, power has different definitions at various stages. I made all the decisions when Wahaha only had 10 people. Things like buying a battery car needed my signature. Now there are more than 260,000 people in the company. My subordinates can sign my names in daily operation. I make the decisions regarding policies, plans, tenders and investments. Wahaha now implements a planning and approval system in which I am responsible for formulating the monthly plan and approving the budget. Now I no longer manage employees, and hand the task over to the management of various levels.

In addition, I will continue to give them directions in the new business. As the development of the company, there is not much problem in maintaining the status quo, but it is difficult to continue to develop at a high speed. Managing business is like going against the water, if you don't advance, you will have to retreat. Each product has its own life cycle, and it will be saturated at a certain time. Therefore, we must constantly find new development points to gain growing acceleration, which calls for continuous innovation. Every time I develop a new product, I will give my subordinates a direction for them to study. We will discuss it again after studying, and I make the final decision. Due to long-term contact with the market, I understand the market demand. Also, savvy is important in doing business, but there are still few people equipped with that quality inside the organization, so I need to take the direction.

CBR: It sounds a bit extreme that you make all the major decisions. It also involves a matter of efficiency in decision making. Has your decision-making method made you pay a price? How to ensure a right decision?

Zong Qinghou: I made the final decision on the basis of full investigation and research in advance, as well as many internal discussions that absorb all useful ideas. So the conclusion demonstrates the group wisdom. For instance, I don't trust the investigation company who investigates the market share by considering the market share of a certain product in the national supermarkets. However, Wahaha's products are less seen in the big supermarkets, since their main channels are small stores and shops. In China, small shops across the street sell the most Wahaha products. When it is hot in summer, the customer can easily buy a bottle of drink produced by Wahaha. Moreover, the large supermarkets are in arrears with the sale fund of the manufacturers, so we don't have much cooperation with them. We will make a mistake by taking the market share of Wahaha's products in big supermarkets as the real market share.

For so many years, I have not made any major mistake. Of course there are certain minor mistakes, which can be corrected in time. One of our strategies is "one small step ahead", according to which, we will first produce a batch of products and put them on the market for testing. If it performs badly, we can stop production immediately; otherwise, we will expand the production scale as soon as possible. The proportion of each new product's sales will not be too large. Big mistakes can be avoided by using such methods.

Of course, at different development stages for enterprises, the meaning of "small step" is different. How big can the step be taken when we only earned ten thousand yuan per year in the beginning? Now we can earn several billion yuan each year, and the decision that is worth tens of millions of yuan does not have much impact on me. Thus, the sales forecast of a newly launched product is usually 2 or 3 billion yuan, since the sales of several hundred million yuan is too small for me.

CBR: According to Kai-Fu Lee, in the process of internal management of enterprises, team is more important than individual; empowerment is more important than command; and equality is more important than authority. What is your opinion?

Zong Qinghou: I agree with the view that "team is more important than individual", but not "empowerment is more important than command". According to my experience of doing business, I don't need to command when the company is in normal operation. But I have to give orders when there is a problem with the company at the critical time. As for equality and authority, I think the latter matters more. For business leaders, it is a terrible thing that no one listens to you. How can we operate the company in a unified way when the organization is a collection of atomized individuals? What can be done without absolute authority?

Moreover, another benefit of absolute authority is that there will be no interest groups that might bring fatal negative impacts. Having more than two interest groups within the company will make it get out of line. There are no interest groups among my subordinates, because I am the only one with the highest authority. If there are two people at the highest level, there will be interest groups that rely on backstage supporters. Without backstage supporters, there will not be interest groups.

CBR: You have a "heroic" leadership style that drives business development with personal authority and capability. Under such leadership, what do you think of your relationship with employees? Can they understand you? Do you know what they want?

Zong Qinghou: Compared with "heroic" leadership style, I think the "paternalistic leadership" is more proper. When the company was small, employees came to me for basically everything, even family affairs. This was true when there were 2,000 employees in our company. Of course, I cannot make contact with every grassroots employee now that there are more than 20,000 employees in Wahahaha. Currently the employees are asking me to work for a few more years, so I am working for them now. Why are they afraid of my retirement? With me, they can have a good life! Ordinary employees who have been in the company for more than a year can buy the company's shares at a price of 1 yuan per share according to their job positions. In the second year, they can receive dividends of 7 cents per share. For many employees, more than 50% of their income comes from dividends. Therefore, they are convinced of my ability. Every employee has thought of the company. During the time when Wahaha and Danone had a business battle, not one employee or dealer turned their coat, and all of them stood firmly on my side. This is very telling.

When I communicated with the middle-level managers, I knew what they were thinking before they finished their words. When I assign heavy responsibility to my employees, I value loyalty first, then integrity, diligence, and intelligence. A base person can never be used.

I think Chinese business leaders need higher emotional intelligence than Western leaders. China enjoys abundant culture due to its long history. People have high IQ and many views, which makes it difficult to unite and manage them. My daughter has encountered this problem. She went to the United States in high school. Now when she comes back to help me with my work, she shows the style of confronting the tough with toughness. In her view, there is a distinctive line between boss and employee. I told her that the way the relationship between the boss and employee is dealt with in the West cannot be completely copied in China. Saving face is still important in China.

CBR: In China, it is often the case that the company takes a bad turn after the capable man leaves. But the mature Western enterprise can continue to develop well after the founder or the capable leaves. What do you think the reason is? Do you think your daughter can be as good as you if she takes over the business in the future?

Zong Qinghou: The Century Enterprise is not only rarely seen in China, but also uncommon in the West. I think all we need is to ensure that the successor is a capable person, no matter if they are my daughter or the management. My core employees are still capable with good executive powers in other companies. For various departments, the heads' abilities to command the overall situation are also improved. No matter who will take over, the successor must have worked in Wahaha for many years instead of the external newcomer who cannot bring the desired results based on my previous experiences.

I am also making some preparations to ensure that Wahaha can continue to survive and develop after my retirement. The first preparation is the standardization of the enterprise. Everyone should know what they are doing and what they need to achieve. It is difficult to quantify the aspect, but we have made gradual progress. The second one is to expand the scale. A larger scale means stronger competitiveness to be better than our competitors. Wahaha's sales last year were 34 billion yuan, and this year we are striving to achieve the sales of 50 billion yuan. The target in the next few years is 100 billion yuan, but it is not big enough. After the scale is large enough, the successor does not need to maintain the current growth rate and the speed of innovation. It will be okay as long as the existing scale is maintained. Also, with a larger scale, more talents will gather in our company, leading to better-trained teams.

CBR: According to the media reports, you are really someone in selling. You have been outside the company for sales promotion more than 200 days a year. Paying attention to every detail of production, you even write the monthly sales reports by yourself. In other words, you have invested great energy in specific sales and production work. So what about the internal management? Can you talk about your management philosophy?

Zong Qinghou: The first step for enterprises to survive is to stress sales. When we make a good job of selling, we will then focus on management and R&D. In Chinese, "management" has two characters, one means "taking charge", the other means "putting everything in order". For me, the most important thing is "putting everything in order". Take less care and put more things in order, and you will find out main threads and make right rules. Then you can ask your subordinates to take charge by telling them how to do it and what to do.

My management philosophy is to make complicated things simple. There are very few basic principles, which requires a great deal of knowledge. Thus, the most important thing is to grasp the essence. I told the CEO of the sales company to solve two problems: Who will help you sell your products? Who will buy your goods? The answer to the first question is to solve the problem of interest distribution with dealers. If selling your product is more profitable than selling someone else's product, dealers will help you sell it. The answer to the second question requires us to provide goods suited to popular tastes, guarantee the product quality, set reasonable prices and fashionable packaging to encourage the consumer to pay the bill. It is as simple as that.

CBR: All of your management philosophy and methods are summed up and explored by yourself. Have you used Western management tools? Are they effective?

Zong Qinghou: We have introduced Systems, Applications & Products in data processing's (SAP) Enterprise Resource Planning (ERP) management system, but found it very difficult to use. The original intention of introducing it was to make the company more standardized. Then we found the financial system one was good, but the supply chain system didn't suit our company. The market is constantly changing, but SAP's system works in an inflexible way. In the past, we fixed output quota by sales, and different branch factories produced different kinds of products. The ERP system searches for information nationwide to determine which supplier provides the specific kind of products, ending up in a total mass. The SAP system is needed and applicable to Western companies that have developed to the highest stage when the company is standardized with stable growth and little changes. But Chinese companies are still in a period of rapid development and are changing too fast, so a complete copy of Western management tools will be doomed to fail.

I have never attended an MBA program or studied any management theory. Western thoughts are summed up based on practice, so it certainly makes some sense, but its problem is to play the game of concepts to make people muddleheaded. For example, what does the "Blue Ocean Strategy" mean? Is there a place without competition in this world? This is nothing more than a change of concept without proposing new things.

CBR: You said that you worshiped Mao Zedong, and *Selected Works of Mao Zedong* has a great influence on you. Can you specifically talk about the impact of Mao Zedong's thoughts on your management methods and leadership style?

Zong Qinghou: When I was working on the farm, I didn't have any other books to read but the *Selected Works of Mao Zedong*. This book really has a great impact on me. How to mobilize the masses to support you? How can you make so many people willingly work hard for you? Human beings are selfish in nature. Only when their various needs are satisfied will they start to consider public interest and reach the ideal phase. So Mao Zedong distributed lands for the peasants, put forward the slogan of "two acres of land, one cow, a wife and children in your home". What a desirable life for the peasants at that time! So Mao was able to rally multitudes at his call and make all water run to his mill. Chiang Kai-shek couldn't figure out why he was not able to beat Mao Zedong. It turned out that he didn't understand the nature of human beings like Mao. This story enlightens me that one must think about how to help others make money when doing business, no matter his employees or dealers. Only when they earn money can you make a profit. This is the nature of business.

Mao Zedong is a military strategist and politician. Doing business is like fighting a battle. Military theory can be used in the field of business and management. For example, many theories proposed by Mao such as "democratic centralism", "decentralize power on minor issues, while centralize power on major issues", "surround the cities from the countryside", and "little chips light great fires" are very helpful to me. I also apply them when doing business. My management philosophy is "democratic centralism" which works well. The reason I developed and launched Feichang Coke is that the urban market is occupied by Coca–Cola and Pepsi. So I started from the rural market, and this method achieved good results.

CBR: You mentioned that you had been working hard on the beverage market for many years. Overall, you are more specialized without engaging in "diversification" strategy. Without bank loans, Wahaha also did not go public. Can you explain these alternative behaviors?

Zong Qinghou: In the past few years, many people advocated that enterprises should promote diversification to put eggs in more than one basket. As a result, these people have messed up the companies. But it is not right to completely refuse diversification. We need to make three judgments: Whether the industry is coming to the end; whether there are new opportunities to develop other industries; and whether the company has the ability to diversify. For example, it is right for Uni-President to adopt a diversification strategy. Since Taiwan has only a population of more than 20 million, how much money can the company make by only selling drinks? Therefore, it has to engage in a variety of industries such as beverages, instant noodles, and eight-treasure porridge. However, in the mainland, enterprises must enlarge the scale of one specific product range before promoting diversification. Otherwise it is hard to succeed. For Wahaha, the beverage industry still has potential for development in the mainland. Nowadays, the per capita consumption of beverages on average in mainland China attains several tens of kilograms, while the number in developed countries is several hundreds of kilograms. This shows that there is large room for growth. On the other hand, I am also focusing on and willing to invest in high-tech, bioengineering, and clean energy industries.

As for the lack of loans, I don't like dealing with banks, which may be the result of the fear of poverty from a young age. Banks treat you kindly when you are rich, and tread on you when you are poor. Also, why need I go public? I have liquid capital of hundred million yuan in the bank. Is it really necessary to go public?

In addition, all the beverage bottles, lids and molds of the products are made by our own company, which can save three-quarter cost compared with buying them from others. When we can make profit from all the links, we will achieve a higher level of profit margin. Are these behaviors alternative? In fact, they are not. We are doing business in a way to make more money. It is quite simple. All the corporate behaviors are based on this basic principle.

About the Author

Zhi Weiyong is senior reporter of the *CEIBS Business Review*. This article was originally published in the 9th issue of the *CEIBS Business Review* in 2009.

XV

Are You a Narcissistic Leader?

Art Kleiner

Anyone who has watched a company go through a change of leadership is keenly aware of how strongly the personality of the chief executive can shape performance. In his 2006 book, *The Leader on the Couch: A Clinical Approach to Changing People and Organizations*, Professor Manfred F. R. Kets de Vries[1] explains the "shadow side of leadership", and how it keeps many companies from realizing their full potential.

Don't be Tolerant of "Destructive Narcissists"

strategy+business (S+B): In *The Leader on the Couch*, you blame the struggles of many companies on their tolerance for narcissistic leaders. How serious a problem is this?

KETS de VRIES: The economic crisis was a reflection of narcissism and very primitive defense mechanisms (such as a complete denial of economic reality) built into the financial system. The best and brightest MBA students have been going into investment banking; many of them used their brains essentially to play casino games, and not to add much value to society. Companies like Citibank — which was the brainchild of

[1] Professor Manfred F. R. Kets de Vries, the Chaired Professor of Leadership Development at INSEAD, has spent much of his academic career on this influential research.

one of the most visibly narcissistic executives in the world, Sanford Weill — have essentially collapsed. No matter what kinds of regulatory reforms are initiated, more companies will collapse this way, because narcissism breeds this kind of unmanageable grandiosity.

S+B: Is that what you mean by narcissism? Grandiosity?

KETS de VRIES: Not exactly. Narcissism is a clinically recognized disorder. In an oversimplified way, it can be viewed as a pathological reaction to problems concerning self-worth. It manifests itself in the need to prove to yourself that you are special and entitled to special treatment. Other indicators include a need for constant attention and admiration, selfishness, a lack of empathy, the exploitation of others, and enviousness.

Narcissistic people may evade rules and regulations; their attitude is that these apply only to others. They may throw tantrums when they don't get their way. Their outbursts of rage can be phenomenal. But some of their behavior can be interpreted by others as quite charismatic. And thus they often rise to lead large organizations and put a strong stamp on them.

Keep in mind that narcissism in and of itself isn't a bad thing; it's part of our makeup. It may have received a bad reputation because of the Greek myth of Narcissus, the youth who fell in love with his reflection. But in moderation, the condition is natural and even necessary. It contributes to assertiveness, self-confidence, and creativity. These are all very desirable qualities for business leaders. People who achieve things — who write books, who run companies, who oversee projects — have to be somewhat narcissistic, or they wouldn't be motivated to excel. Some of our most gifted leaders have evident narcissism. John Harvey-Jones, for instance, the head of Imperial Chemical Industries [ICI] during the 1980s and host of a BBC television show called Troubleshooter in the 1990s, was a charismatic individual, with wild eyes, wild ties, and wild hair. He was also a consummate, constructive narcissist.

But narcissistic people in elevated positions can be destructive. When they reach the highest echelons, given their need for positive mirroring, those who work for them start to tell them what they want to hear. They lose their sense of reality. And then their narcissism needs to be harnessed.

Impostor Syndrome

S+B: But what about the humble, responsible, very capable people who cope with enormous pressure and keep their heads? Haven't you met many such people in business?

KETS de VRIES: Certainly. Most people in corporations are like that. Many of them have a solid dose of humanity, humility, and humor. If you can still make fun of yourself, that's a good sign of mental health. In an overly simplistic way, you can divide humanity into three groups. The first group, about 20 percent, has been lucky in life. They had a reasonably happy background. Take for example Richard Branson, the chairman of the Virgin Group, about whom I have written many case studies. I even interviewed his parents once; he had a very warm father and an entrepreneurial, supportive mother. He is an example of the kind of person who feels very good in his skin. At the other extreme, 20 percent have suffered through a difficult childhood. When children grow up neglected, too pampered, or treated as an extension of their parents, they can lose their ability to relate their internal image of themselves to the real world outside them. As they grow into adults, they find it hard to maintain a stable sense of self-esteem. The pursuit of admiration, of feeling important, may turn into a lifelong quest. They're determined to prove that they amount to something. Some of these people respond, given what they experienced, by adopting destructive character traits. And then the middle 60 percent, from a clinical point of view, can be described as mildly neurotic. That's hopefully us!

Some people, in these latter two groups, hold the attitude that life is tough, and they have to take for themselves everything they can. They may even turn spiteful and vindictive. Others say, "Listen, I have had a hard time, but I want to rise above it. I want to do something different, or give something back." That is the group I most admire. They try to change things for the better, starting with themselves. And if they become leaders, they have an impact on their companies. In the political world, these are the Gandhis and Mandelas.

S+B: How do businesses end up with so many destructive narcissists in charge?

KETS de VRIES: Many successful people in business can be described as insecure overachievers. They feel like they're fakes; that it could be discovered that they don't actually know what they're doing as managers. This is known as the "impostor syndrome," and it's quite common. Whatever they accomplish, they feel it is never good enough. It may start when they are tapped to lead others.

And if you rise to run a company of, say, 100,000 people, naturally you wonder sometimes, "Do I really deserve this position?" You'd be very unusual if you felt otherwise. But you'd have to be quiet about it, because if anyone found out you felt like an impostor, they would question why you were there, in that role, making so much money. Some people compensate for this feeling of insecurity by becoming more narcissistic: convincing themselves, and everyone else, that they truly are special.

S+B: Presumably, the higher they get, the more the rest of the company contributes to this.

KETS de VRIES: Exactly. Harvey-Jones tells the story that when he became the chairman of ICI, he wanted to continue to drive to work in his old, battered Volkswagen. But he was told subtly to stop such nonsense. The chairman of ICI is supposed to arrive in a Rolls-Royce, driven by a chauffeur. He had a good sense of how ridiculous this was; others easily get used to it. They start to believe that they are entitled to such things — and more.

Your natural narcissism is combined with being in a top position, and before you know it, you live in a hall of mirrors. People always agree with you. You see what you want to see. It's very difficult to resist becoming grandiose. And suddenly you're finished. You lose the ability to realize your ambitions for the company.

Alexander the Great, for example, was somewhat of a participative manager in his early life. He got his key people — his "companions", as they were known — very much involved in decision making. But as he entered his late 20s, he started to believe that he was a god. That was the end of his participative management period. Because he died so young, we will never really know how he would have ended up.

It's still very hard for senior executives to get frank feedback — or to welcome it. I worked with a corporate leader from the Caucasus who got a perfect score in his subordinates' appraisals of him. They said he was a great manager. Then I found out that he had handed out the feedback forms to his subordinates with their names printed on them, and said, "Bring these back to my office." This case may be extreme, but that's the kind of feedback that many leaders get. There's the famous scene in Joseph Heller's Catch-22 where Lieutenant Scheisskopf says, "I'll be grateful to the man who tells me the truth," and then court-martials the one person who dares to speak up.

Companies without Narcissistic Leaders

S+B: Do all companies breed narcissism in this way?

KETS de VRIES: No. Some companies are what I call "authentizotic", meaning that people are attracted to work for them. These organizations cultivate three major values.

The first is a sense of meaning: People feel they do something substantial. For instance, Novo Nordisk, a Danish pharmaceutical manufacturer, is in the insulin business. People are not likely to go on strike there because they know what will happen to their customers. Another example is the National Australia Bank. It was originally a farmers' bank, and senior executives in this company pride themselves that very few farmers went bankrupt during the recent financial crisis. They are in for the long haul.

The second value is a feeling of being a family. Take W.L. Gore, which is probably one of the most creative companies in America. The family ethos is very important in this firm. Richard Branson's Virgin Group works the same way. He has gone to great lengths to maintain this family feeling.

Then there is the quality of fun, or enjoyment, in the work itself.

S+B: What else do you suggest to leaders who are trying to move to more authentizotic behavior?

KETS de VRIES: If a person has a narcissistic personality, that individual is always going to be somewhat narcissistic, but he or she can learn to become more aware of the results of such behavior. Imagine that you have an elephant inside you. The elephant is a metaphor for your inner theater, your personality. You can nudge it a little bit, but you cannot make it go away. Sigmund Freud used to talk about having a wild horse inside us, but I think the elephant is a better metaphor. It lumbers around inside and it doesn't forget.

I also suggest that when executives become the king or the queen of the castle, they need to create an environment where people will have a healthy disrespect for the boss. There should be an open give and take, with no penalties for venturing a different opinion. We don't want leaders like Lieutenant Scheisskopf. Some great executives choose to have people working for them whom the French sometimes call a morosoph: a "wise fool" — the fool of Shakespeare's King Lear. These people can raise difficult issues in a joking way. Of course, they may go too far and get "killed" eventually. For example, when I go to Russia to work with senior executives, I often take on the role of the wise fool. I may walk in the snow and talk about the meaning of life, and sometimes when the timing is right, I say something that really sets the person thinking.

How to Move Away from Narcissism

S+B: What is the role of leadership development programs in helping executives move away from narcissism?

KETS de VRIES: The challenge is to help them open up and trust each other, to create an ambiance of social reciprocity, to take some risks together. I've seen this done extremely well within many companies in their learning programs or change efforts. But to be really effective, you need to start with the top executives, because they're the ones who have influence, and then move down the hierarchy to other decision makers. I remember talking to Jorma Ollila when he was the CEO at Nokia [he is now the non-executive chairman of both Nokia and Royal Dutch Shell] about the executive leadership workshops there. I said, "You know, the first time you attend such a workshop, it's fun. But are you going to be there the 20th time?" He said, "I will still be there." It was important because of the signal it would send to the attendees. And he delivered.

Leadership development programs provide an opportunity for a group of very senior executives to talk, in a fairly informal environment, with their peers about complex organizational and personal issues. Many of them start off with a question like: "I've been the CEO of this bank for a number of years. Is this all I want — to be the richest person in the graveyard? What can I do to renew myself?"

During the seminar, they get a better understanding of their leadership style, and how they come across to others. It is also a good opportunity to work on their emotional intelligence. They start to become more reflective in action on a day-to-day basis. This means they think more and say, "What am I doing — and why am I doing it?" before they act.

In the process of giving feedback to each other, they become more effective leaders. They begin to use themselves as an instrument. They listen to the text of what people say and the music — the words and their unspoken meaning. Very often, the feedback from people close to them, like their children, has the greatest effect on them. If your grown daughter is not approving of you, you start moving.

It's not one of those short seminars where people exit with a eureka feeling, and soon go back to normal. This elephant inside you is very large. You can't remove it in a few days. By the last week, I'm always quite impressed by the kind of changes the participants have made, both in their business and in their private lives. I am also very pleased with the way they deal with each other. They're less self-centered; they start to realize the complexity and value of other people. They have courageous conversations with people at work and at home. And they have truly committed to reinventing the way they do things.

It turns out this is what senior executives want most. They don't really want to be exposed to more economic models; they want to think about the direction of their lives. And since many of them are responsible for thousands of people, what they learn may have a beneficial broader effect.

S+B: Are most managers prepared for this type of self-awareness?

KETS de VRIES: Not at first. But after a while, they discover that they are not alone in their confusion. It's been evident for a long time that many people, as they move on in their careers, become more interested in longer-term issues. They may start out influenced by money, perhaps if they were poor as children. They may then become obsessed by spending power, by what Thorstein Veblen called conspicuous consumption. Who can afford to buy the biggest car, house, or yacht? But eventually they realize that however rich they get, someone will always be richer. So they start to try to do something for society, something meaningful.

And it's barely possible that the same may be true for business people as a whole. In our "Consulting and Coaching for Change" class — which consists of a mixed group of people, including line managers, HR professionals, consultants, and executive coaches — we play a simulation game. It's set on an island like Jamaica, with a large population under the poverty line. Teams of players represent a bank, a group of radical activists, an investor consortium, a hotel owner, and a group that wants to start an airline. And, of course, there is a team that plays the role of the government. The island's economy collapses. As the situation gets tougher, people typically begin to pull fast ones on each other, trying to get any advantage they can. The hotel group tries to sell at an exploitive price; the radicals start rioting. And the bank pulls back its lending. It becomes a zero-sum game. But this year, the outcome was quite different. The players took a much broader perspective, and started designing a solution together that would be better for the island as a whole.

It was striking that in the debrief, when I asked why they picked that strategy, the participants said, "Listen, given the economic state of the world, and the state of the environment, it would be better to look at the long run."

Ten years ago, people in business schools talked only about short-term gains and the value of being purely rational. It's very fortunate for me, because these students continue to help me discover my ignorance.

About the Author

Art Kleiner is editor-in-chief of the *strategy+business* quarterly magazine. This article was originally published in the 6th issue of *CEIBS Business Review* in 2010.

XVI

Thinking Map for Leaders

S. Ramnarayan, Sudhanshu Palsule and Manoj Pawar

As a business leader, do you understand the "thinking map" behind your decision-making behavior? Management scholars S. Ramnarayan, Sudhanshu Palsule and Manoj Pawar started an interesting discussion regarding this issue. The specific topics include: What new implications of modern research on the brain for leadership behavior? How will traditional wisdom change team dynamics? What is the important role of psychological intervention in improving leadership?

Awareness and Choice

Ramnarayan: Are awareness and choice making equally important for leaders as well as teams?

Pawar: Emotions, rationality, and spirituality — all three contexts play an important role in a leader's decision-making process. When a leader is unaware that he/she is relying totally on one versus the other, problems arise. Emotional intelligence means awareness and appropriate use of emotion, not suppression. In some instances, say in crisis management, well thought-out protocols, when accurately executed, are appropriate. For more complex decisions, it would be wrong to respond with a reaction based on what has been done in the past. Our reptilian brain remembers the previous time something was done; it may not be appropriate to repeat the action just because it "feels" somehow right.

Instinct as a source of wisdom is also important to tap into. It gets forgotten or is not valued in organizational contexts. Malcolm Gladwell's book *Blink* discusses this. We don't know yet if the reptilian brain is involved in intuition, but the parietal lobes of the brain are. When we experience a sensory input one can choose how to react to it. We have an opportunity to say "I know I am feeling this way, I am going to give it a chance, I will take a deep breath, and shift towards curiosity and exploration as opposed to action." Time spent in reflection, silence, meditation, is very helpful.

When a leader intuitively senses something, he can choose to suspend an immediate decision and ask the team to discuss it further, even if there may be tension or disagreement over an issue. A leader can use silence effectively, to signal deep thinking or disagreement etc. Sometimes silence can create a degree of tension, which in turn can raise awareness. Assuming that the leader has created an environment of trust, they can share misgivings or admit to limitations, and the anxiety that triggers the stress or survival response of flight or fight can be appeased amongst team members. It can shift from defensiveness into curiosity, learning, understanding the root cause.

Chemically, you can avoid the surge of adrenalin which increases the heart rate, shallow breathing, etc.

Ramnarayan: Have studies been done on individuals and teams in situations of trust and mistrust?

Pawar: For individuals, yes. I give a few examples. Like an electroencephalogram (EEG), which measures the brain wave and the electrical activity of different parts of the brain during different situations; biofeedback, which looks at the conductivity of the skin surface, sweating, temperature, pulse rate, blood pressure, breathing, etc. They can be indirect indicators of how much stress the individual is experiencing at the time. Functional magnetic resonance imaging (fMRI), a very powerful but expensive tool, shows which parts of the brain are activated during certain situations.

Emotion Motivates Reform

Ramnarayan: Is motivation or believing in the cause more important for bringing about organizational change than just the reasons for change?

Palsule: I have found in my research that if people are not included in the change process, the biology of the brain responds very much in the same way that it responded to danger 45,000 years ago. Biochemically, the brain cannot tell the difference between organizational change and an approaching tiger.

Pawar: When you are included, you identify with what is being created; there is safety in that. You are activating the pre-frontal areas of the brain. If you are not included, there is resistance, stress, maybe sabotage. Emotion is the fuel for change. Consider an organization as a living entity; a certain degree of stress is necessary for any living organism to adapt. Without that the organism becomes vulnerable. The leader's job is to convey that in a healthy fashion. The emerging role of a 21st century leader is really "sense-making".

Ramnarayan: Leaders know that it is essential for people to feel included, yet my research shows that it is precisely what leaders don't do. Is there a neurological explanation to that?

Palsule: Many leaders suffer from attention deficit disorder. Their stress levels are high, the executive brain which is responsible for making sure that people are included, is sub-optimized. It is not done diabolically or deliberately, leaders are not conscious about it. I read that the average time a CEO spends making a decision is probably thirty seconds.

Make Good Use of Self-Consciousness

Ramnarayan: Power plays an important role. Successful people may want centrality most of the time. Do they want to share the glory?

Palsule: Ego blinds you. It sub-optimizes perception. The brain probably sees it similar to a stress situation. Manoj talks about peer-stress, which is where the brain gets distorted and you don't see things that are in front of you, and as a result business leaders end up making faulty decisions.

Pawar: Part of the leader's job is to perceive reality as it happens. But when ego and desire come into play there is a distortion of reality. This is where wisdom traditions give us more insight. *The Geeta* says you must do your duty but you don't have any right to the fruits of that.

Ramnarayan: If I were not cognizant of the fruit of my labor, why would I start in the first place? There seems to be a gap in the interpretation of this oft-quoted verse from *The Geeta*.

Pawar: Part of your concentration is wasted in paying attention to immediate rewards. It has something to do with the reward mechanism in our brain. If I am not attached to the fruit of the labor, the brain moves on to a long-term reward mechanism.

Palsule: The more you want it, the more likely you worry about it, and the more likely you are going to make a mistake. Perhaps that was the original intent of that phrase. As a coach I know that it takes a long time for CEOs to get over their sense of self-importance. The more I spend time with people at the top, the more I realize that they are much more insecure than the people below. Also, because they are in denial, it makes it worse. Coaching is very helpful.

Pawar: When you see a patient with diabetes for the first time, you look at the test results and know that if some lifestyle changes are not done, this person is in serious danger. But you can't say, "I am the one that knows what is best for you." You have to build trust first. Then you have to match where they are currently. That may mean sacrificing your desires to move forward as a coach, but it is important to meet the person where they are at, know what is important to them, what are their drivers, etc.

Ramnarayan: After someone learns to deal with fear, anxiety etc., would he/she be able to continue effectively at work without further coaching?

Palsule: You have to be prepared to observe yourself and become more aware of things as they happen, not retrospectively. People are inherently suited to do this themselves. They don't need a coach. A coach is simply a mirror in which you can see yourself. More importantly, people develop through relationships. Every relationship shows us where we are lacking. Sometimes we are blind to our behaviors; what we may consider as our strengths, somebody else from another perspective may think otherwise.

Pawar: There is a lot of power in the questions we ask ourselves, in listening to the talk we have inside of our brains, in being honest with ourselves. We love to collude; we may not want to see ourselves the way we actually are. A good relationship can help in reflecting the real you.

Ramnarayan: Can one's boss be your coach or does it have to be someone external? The boss is also an evaluator.

Pawar: It is possible for a boss to have coach-like behaviors. But ulterior motives can be a danger. It is a tricky situation.

Palsule: Performance evaluation and coaching are at loggerheads with each other. It is a conflict of interest, unless you have a truly enlightened boss, which is very rare.

Change Behavior Pattern

Ramnarayan: We talked about effective conversations, about helping people getting in touch, becoming aware, and about choice-making ability. Can you share some instances which conveyed these messages powerfully to people?

Pawar: Two examples come to mind. I had a patient who was dying and her family was quarrelling over what should be done for her. Everybody was getting angry. I focused the conversations to explain that ultimately the individual wants dignity and happiness. All of a sudden the self-interest of the family members washed away.

In an organizational context, I had an ex-military commander as a client, he was a command-and control type. However, he struggled with a younger workforce with very different expectations. We did a lot of exercises together. I made him visualize certain situations and observe his reactions — "Imagine this person telling you this, do you feel your hands getting moist, do you feel your heart rate going up?" Then we interrupted that neural path and did something different like a breathing task. Over time he was able to repeat that in real life situations — breaking the old neural paths and the patterns of behavior. The big test for him was to have a conversation with one particular individual he had alienated, and in the course of that conversation tell him to manage his anger. He surprised me by changing himself. You experience magic when groups of people finally learn to have conversations with each other that are hard and painful, and eventually start performing together.

Ramnarayan: Can you elaborate on how one can break a pattern of behavior?

Palsule: There are some people whose self-awareness is in reasonably good shape, but they never learned some basic behaviors. Working on self-awareness is a long-term process. Often it takes a lifetime; it is not easy. But you can simultaneously work on your behavior. Let me take the cue from sports psychology. If Tiger Woods has had a couple of bad swings on a day in the green, he will make it a point that evening to go back on the green and keep swinging until he finds the right swing. He knows that his muscle memory is critical. When he comes back the next day his muscles have to pick up that good swing and not the bad swing. You can actually change behavior by replacing it with something else. Do something different and then do it again and again. It is like behavioral therapy in psychology where you actively and consciously disrupt a pattern which has forced the brain to go into the default way of doing things you have done for twenty years. And that can be fun. People can take control of that process.

Ramnarayan: You talked about leaders feeling insecure.

Palsule: In my research, during the last five years, I have found that the one emotion that we do not acknowledge enough in our corporations is "fear". Fear is a rampant emotion in companies, it is pervasive and deep, and senior executives have tremendous amount of fear. Once that takes root, it brings up all the other smaller emotions into play.

Ramnarayan: What are the reasons for fear in a corporate situation other than risky business strategies or failure?

Palsule: It is not the fear of not knowing whether I will succeed or not, it is a fear of not being included. It is a fear of feeling ostracized, a fear of not having enough knowledge about things.

Fear is a signal; it is important to find what it is pointing to. It may be a threat to the way somebody perceives himself. In another case it may be that the individual is so comfortable in a particular state that any change is fearful. Lack of self-esteem causes fear. Am I good enough or not? People who have made it into the executive team still have doubts about being good enough. Emotions are part of the same vicious cycle; a problem in one immediately affects all the others. For most people it may not be felt at a conscious level. The first step is to be aware of the fear, and to not let it paralyze you. But when fear becomes pathological as a stress response, it sets in for everything that happens at all times. It becomes a default mechanism. How do you tell somebody not to be scared? The pre-frontal cortex is no longer working, the fear is so deep. In such times it is better to use behavioral psychology to tackle the problem.

About the Authors

S. Ramnarayan is Clinical Professor of Organizational Behavior at the Indian School of Business (ISB) and Member of the Management Council of ISB's Centre for Leadership, Innovation, and Change (CLIC). **Sudhanshu Palsule** is Visiting Professor at the Helsinki School of Economics and the ISB. **Manoj Pawar** is Adjunct Professor at the University of Denver.

XVII

Peter Senge: The Era of Global Corporations is Coming to an End

Piao Baoyi

Social Learning is Essential

CBR: You mentioned the importance of the systemic thinking for leaders in *The Fifth Discipline: The Art and Practice of the Learning Organization*. Chinese entrepreneur Liu Chuanzhi also talked about the importance of stepping back to look at the picture clearly. But you also mentioned that we often saw part of the picture even when stepping back to expand our horizons. The reason is that people always focus on one or two of their personal preferences and observe the changes of their focuses. What should leaders do to change this situation?

Peter Senge: I agree with Mr. Liu's view that "it is essential to step back to look at the picture clearly". One of the most effective ways to help people truly understand a larger system is through a "learning journey", a way that allows people to look at all aspects of a larger system in a team environment to have personally experience how they are interrelated. This first-hand experience is crucial to help us get out of the habitual thinking, evoke feelings or emotions, and boost understanding through numbers and concepts. In the process of exploring interdependence, combining skills with concepts can generate rich and derivable ideas in larger systems. Sometimes they can be very confusing, because we know that it is impossible for one person to see the entire content of "a larger system". Blind spots cannot be avoided, making us unable to see the key features of a larger system.

Frankly speaking, nothing can guarantee us to grasp the whole picture. No one has ever seen all aspects of reality or a system. The key is to understand some important issues from the level of a larger system to learn more aspects related to the facts. In this sense, all the systematic thinking is focused on certain well-defined issues.

CBR: A sound mind plays an extremely important role in personal decision-making. The *CEIBS Business Review* has introduced "mindfulness", a tool of Buddhist Zen, to help leaders to look at their relationship with the environment in a "detaching" attitude. Mindfulness can help leaders avoid falling into the intrinsic mode of thinking and habitual impulses. This has something in common with your views, like "to clearly see the structure behind the complex situation", "to deal with the external causes as internal reasons", and "to avoid the simple thinking mode of 'stress-response'". Can you talk about how you cultivate your mind?

Peter Senge: People have a common understanding of the importance of reflection, because the operating mechanism of human consciousness and the problems encountered by people are interlinked. Therefore, it is not surprising to see that some of the ideas formed from long-term traditions (like Buddhist Zen) can also be seen in other fields, such as effective interpersonal communication, and sound judgment on right or wrong. For me, my thinking ability is usually developed in the process of dealing with people. In fact, in daily life, there are always people who have completely different views to challenge my views on how to perceive the world. If I can learn to regard their views as catalysts for thinking, there will be many opportunities for reflection on my life. In addition, I have the habit of meditation, which allows me to control my consciousness more deeply to make my physical and mental state calmer and more harmonious.

Entrepreneurs always have a question, "What can I do to change my behavior?" "How can I change my hidden beliefs?" People often want a formula, technique or tangible thing to solve structural conflicts. But when they rack their brains to find a solution, they tend to ignore the most powerful strategy, which is to honestly face the truth. It sounds simple, but it may be the most difficult thing.

CBR: Why does it sound easy to face the truth honestly, but it is quite difficult in real life? How can we do it?

Peter Senge: We are not saints. Engaged in activities within our own sphere, we hold views that are shaped by our beliefs. However, we all have blind spots, which makes social learning essential. In order to build an atmosphere which encourages honesty among people, it is necessary to create a social environment full of trust. People need to feel that they are "connected to each other." Each of us has shortcomings that can only be effectively compensated by coordination and complementarity to help us borrow others' skills. Therefore, in the real sense, telling the truth is not only a social process, but an individual process. I often see this happening when the team really starts to get fruitful. At first, some people are so worried and anxious that they try to seek self-protection. However, when they truly understand each other in terms of their shared vision, some people will soon begin to break the ice by sharing their fears, anxiety, and uncertainty to deal with the reality. This naturally leads to a resonance of human psychological reactions and a desire to help each other. In this case, people begin to develop the ability to tell the truth.

Motivation Comes from People's Real Wish

CBR: The third discipline you proposed is "to establish a shared vision", with the premise of "individualism", a manifestation of personal values based on which to seek common ground while reserving differences. What is the difference between the third discipline and the "collectivism", "corporate vision" that has traditionally been valued in Chinese society? Will the learning organization dominated by centralized leadership and pyramidal organizational structure be unacceptable in China?

Peter Senge: This is a very complicated question that cannot be explained in a few words. First, I believe that the functions of all organizations are the result of interactions among the various levels and the network. No single work can be completed by simply following the rules, and no hierarchical structure can take complete control. As for whether the third discipline can reach a balance between cultivating personal ideals and building a common vision, and whether it can be compared with China's "collectivism", I think they largely depend on people's efforts to achieve this harmonious condition. I believe it is possible. In my views, all work must be carried out through subtle interactions between individuals, teams (formal and informal), networks, and formal management structures. In this regard, China is no different from other countries, except that the nature and operation of the hierarchy in China are different. China emphasizes the unity of leadership, the role of "leader", and the people at the top. Although this approach is not unique, the country has a unique way of operation. I believe that we must revitalize China's fine traditions and provide a solid foundation for individual development and personal vision to establish a new balance in China. If vitality can be motivated, and a positive atmosphere can be built in the organization, I think a healthy symbiotic relationship can be re-established between individuals and groups, although this may take decades or even generations.

CBR: Based on your observation, most visions are personal beliefs imposed on the organization. This kind of vision is a mere way to win obedience, not represent the genuine pursuit of members. In comparison, a shared vision is something that group members truly pursue. In fact, imposing visions is also common in Chinese companies. But the challenge is how to make group members truly pursue the vision pursued by leaders.

Peter Senge: In my opinion, the problem is not how to make team members truly obey the vision made by others, but to build a shared vision. The two things are different. It is often the case that the "common vision" is simply a person's own vision imposed on others, but the common goal can indeed change history. I do not intend to negate the important role of the one or two people in formulating and launching a vision. They are symbolic formulators of vision standards. The significance of formulating a vision lies in the process rather than the actual result. When people really have their own dreams and are willing to do their best to achieve it, the shared vision will appear. With shared visions, even if "leaders" leave the organization and lose power, people will not stop working. Instead, they will continue to pursue this vision that represents their dreams. At this time, people voluntarily match their actions with a shared vision, rather than passively obey others' visions. People's motivation comes from their true nature and real wishes.

CBR: You mentioned that most people grow up in an authoritative environment. In childhood, they listen to their parents; as students, they listen to their teachers; in the work organization, they listen to their boss. People are taught that those at the higher level know what to do and how to do it, and they think it is true. This mentality hinders the developmental potential of individuals and organizations. However, by observing Chinese companies, I find that the mechanism for one-person decision-making is still dominant. The ups and downs and strategies of enterprises are in the hands of key figures. They cannot question their motives, otherwise the team will not be able to move forward. What should such company leaders do?

Peter Senge: My understanding is that it is very common for one person to decide everything in China. They don't tolerate challenges or doubts due to the concerns that the group will lose a clear direction. I think this thought will eventually become a self-limiting act. Perhaps such an approach may produce a positive outcome when there is an urgent need for decision-making. However, collective wisdom is irreplaceable if a group needs to innovate, or propose a new solution, or create a new source of value. In this sense, in China, the practice of giving orders and directing collective behavior by a certain leader may be just a transitional stage. Along this direction, they will truly develop the ability to tap collective wisdom in the future. I believe that such collective wisdom is of great significance for solving some important issues in China, such as to speed up to get transition to alternative energy.

The Era of Giant Companies is Coming to an End

CBR: The industrial era characterized by large-scale production, competitiveness through scale, and authoritative leadership is over. You also said that we are entering a new era that has not yet been named. Can we call it the "Wiki Economy Era"? If this era is characterized by large-scale collaboration, openness, equivalence, shares, and global operations, what changes must be made by business leaders in terms of their leadership?

Peter Senge: I believe that the character of the era we are entering lies in the historical premise of achieving a balance between human life and the nature world, which is far more important than the role of new information technology and the "Wiki Economy". However, extensive cooperation and openness are extremely important to make the required reform and implement a real ecological model. Therefore, only when we realize once again that human beings are part of the natural world rather than its opposites can humans and nature achieve mutual development.

CBR: Chris Anderson, Editor-in-Chief of *The Economist* and *Wired*, proposes that today one of the main trends is the smaller scale in companies and fewer multinational companies that will make less profit when their scale is bigger. What do you think of this view? How should companies downsize?

Peter Senge: I think the era of giant global companies is likely to come to an end soon, just as many other characteristics of the industrial age have. People have to accept that it might lead to a reduction in profit. How can companies downsize? They can start from focusing on how to get things done, which cannot be achieved through a large scale or a single business department. The current goals can be achieved through teamwork, social network, and collaboration among people. In this process, reforms can be undertaken to set new goals. In many aspects, large global organizations are more like accounting entities rather than actual social systems, because they often contain many different cultures and structures with unique skills and business priorities. In this sense, it is more about focusing on how to get things done to change from big to small.

About the Author

Piao Baoyi is senior editor of *CEIBS Business Review*. This article was originally published in the 2nd issue of the *CEIBS Business Review* in 2010.

XVIII

Today's Stable World is Dangerous: Dialogue with Jim Collins

Stephen Bernhut

Ivey Business Journal (IBJ): Why did you write *How the Mighty Fall*?

Jim Collins (JC): I was interested in why some companies decline, even some of the great companies we wrote about in *Good to Great*. We'd actually been researching the subject of why companies fail for several years. It's important to point out that we were doing this well before the failure of the Wall Street firms just over a year ago. In fact, the book is not about the capital markets at all. It's about giving readers some very revealing and pointed research on how and why decline occurs, and what lessons leaders can learn that will help them avoid the fate of those that did fall.

IBJ: Can you describe the five stages of decline?

JC: Stage One is what we call Hubris Born of Success. Successful companies can become very insulated by their success. People start coasting and saying things like "We're successful because we do these specific things." They forget that they became successful because they understood why they do these specific things and under what conditions they would no longer work. That sort of understanding and insight get replaced by the rhetoric of success. This is the beginning of decline.

Stage Two, what we call Undisciplined Pursuit of More, is basically a continuation of Stage One. Companies forget about what made them successful in the first place and make undisciplined leaps into areas where they can't be great. Leaders want more scale, more growth, more acclaim. Essentially they're overreaching.

In Denial of Risk and Peril, Stage Three, leaders start to discount negative data and begin to blame external factors for setbacks rather than accept responsibility. They start to take huge risks and act in a way that denies the consequences of those risks. This kind of behavior leads straight to Stage Four, Grasping for Salvation.

In Stage Four, the leader, already in trouble, opts for a bold but untested strategy or a blockbuster product launch to pull his or her company out of the freefall. These may work at first but neither strategy will pull the company up for good.

The final stage of decline, Stage Five, is Capitulation to Irrelevance or Death. Financial strength and the company's spirit have been so eroded that leaders abandon all hope. A great icon has become irrelevant. It can take as long as ten years for a company to decline, but it can also take less than a year.

IBJ: What are the most telling indicators that a company is in decline even though it's a market leader?

JC: The number one indicator that I would track is the percentage of key seats that are filled with either competent people or the right people. If that percentage is in decline, you may well be a market leader with tremendous growth potential. But you may also be in Stage Four.

IBJ: If you're in Stage Four, on the edge of the abyss, what can a leader do to pull the company back and up?

JC: It's interesting and I didn't write this in the text strongly because I didn't want it to sound wrong, and I didn't want it to sound like this is an advertisement for *Good to Great*. What do I really believe based on having looked at the pattern of what Gerstner did, or Ann Mulcahy (Xerox)?

First of all, I believe that, based on the evidence, "great degrading to good to bad and returning to great" is not that much different of a process than good to great. And that you still see the emergence of the basic pattern of the disciplined people who are engaged in disciplined thought, take disciplined action. They get the right people first, they confront the brutal facts, they rethink, "Where can we truly be the best and distinctive with great passion, how do we build a culture of discipline around it, how do we rebuild, step by step, the flywheel (*Good to Great*) and how do we do that in a way that is really married to the values that made us great, that we had great allegiance to in the first place?"

And I think that that basic chain still very much applies. It's still an inflection, but it's just a steeper inflection. Instead of an inflection of flat to rising, it's decline to rising, once you've solved the bleeding. The only real difference is that you may have to do some fairly dramatic things at the start to stop the bleeding. I just got an e-mail from somebody who said, "Our company was in decline, I was the CEO, and I recognize now, in retrospect, that we were grasping for salvation. It was finally when I just said, 'We need to really go back to our fundamental disciplines, we need to pull out our (Michael) Porter and see what the real sources of our competitive advantage are, what are the places where we have actual power in this market? How do we bring that power to bear? What are the ways that we slice that out?'" So, you start taking pages from Drucker and you start taking pages from these really fundamental, disciplined approaches to things. Those are largely the answers, the idea that what you have to do is come out and do something utterly dramatic and transformational. And though you end up with something that is transformed, the process is very pedestrian. And that's what I think is so striking about the Gerstner story. What he did was so pedestrian.

IBJ: Can you give a specific description how to start over at this stage?

JC: To create a whole new life and then you infuse that into creating companies and to creating value and so forth. The second thing is this young generation of people that's coming up. At one point on my visit to

West Point earlier this year, the Chief of Staff of the Army said that this is the most inspired and inspiring generation to come to West Point since 1945. And I look at this young generation and I look at leaders like Wendy Kopp (Teach for America) and I look at some of the people building companies. I don't know what's going to happen to the largest companies in America, but this young generation is very inspired. I find them very inspiring. I find them wanting to create movements. I find them wanting to create entire systems that work.

I see people like Wendy Kopp wanting to tackle the biggest problems in our society, doing it through an enterprise. I see people wanting to start companies that do things. Yes, we stumble forward. It's what we do but we always have a young generation and an immigrant generation that comes in and creates stuff and makes stuff happen. Do I have any gloom at all, long-term gloom, meaning the next 100 or 50 years, about America, and its strength? I think we're going to be severely tested. But we're good when we're tested. That's when we're really, really good. I grew up in an era where we weren't particularly tested. But even so, I think, "Boy, we know how to do well when we're tested."

Achieve Excellence in the Volatile Situation

IBJ: Moving away from the book, you've recently been saying that volatility is here to stay. Why do you say that?

JC: Those of us who grew up between 1950 and 2000 grew up in a world defined by two, and then one, superpowers. When you think about it, we grew up in a period of really remarkable prosperity, the '50s, the '60s. We stumbled a bit in the '70s, but then you had this almost unblemished run, really extraordinary run, from the early '80s, after the early '80s recession, to 2000. So you had a period of stability brought about by the presence of two monolithic superpowers, then one, combined with a period of extraordinary prosperity.

If we look back at history, that's more aberrant than normal. There are few times in human history when you have that degree of inherent-seeming stability. I think it was a very dangerous world, a little bit like living in San Francisco, right? There's an earthquake fault that could go at any time, but so long as it doesn't, the weather's pretty nice. And I think that that's kind of the world we grew up in. And I think that the likelihood is that we will return — this is my own view and no one can predict the future — but the likelihood is that we'll return to the historical norm of higher degrees of uncertainty and higher degrees of instability. So the likelihood is that we'll have prosperity. We know how to create that and there's no reason to believe we will fail to create prosperity. But the idea of prosperity and stability prevailing at the same time is probably less likely. So in that sense, I think it's more likely that we will live in a much more uncertain and tumultuous time than those years of prosperity and stability.

IBJ: What makes a merely good leader great today, especially in a time of turbulence?

JC: We've actually been studying that and the next piece of work to come out, probably in a few years, will look explicitly at the question of why some leaders are able to transition from a position of vulnerability to build something great in a world spinning out of control … how they end up in ultimate control, having more control of their own destiny and what separates the leaders who build enterprises that do that.

There's certainly nothing in our prior research that's negated by this research. In other words, they're the leaders who are long-term ambitious for their companies first and foremost, more than for themselves. That still holds, even in this kind of environment. But what gets added to it is the need for a kind of productive paranoia, and the recognition that you have to be constantly vigilant and fearful of the things that might get you. And you don't know what they are. I guess I would describe it as being vigilantly prepared for what you cannot ever possibly predict. And recognizing that if the world is going to throw a lot of stuff at you, you have to prepare ahead of time for the things that are going to hit you and you don't know what they are going to be. That involves a whole series of decisions that you made before you get hit.

Are you conservative financially? Do you have slack and buffers in your system? Do you not grow too fast in good times? So that when you're hit with a really tumultuous time, you've got a little slack in the system to take advantage of it rather than having to feel like, "Oops, we went too far and we need to retrench."

IBJ: What do you do during the positive times?

JC: For example, take a company like Southwest Airlines. One thing that is very interesting is that Southwest has grown up in an environment characterized by tumult. Yet every time the airline industry would go through one of its great retrenchment exercises or difficult periods, Southwest would historically gain position, gain share and make it stronger.

And you have to ask the question, "Why?" And the reason is because during the times when it would be in a more positive environment, not during a recession, not during a war, not post-911, Southwest was very deliberate and disciplined, so it only opened as many cities as it could. It preserved its model and preserved its culture and made sure it had a really strong balance sheet. It was always, always fearful about what could happen. And then when those times would come, they were in a much stronger position and they could take advantage of other people's weaknesses.

Never Stop Asking Questions

IBJ: I've read that you favor using the Socratic Method for getting to the bottom of things, asking a lot of questions. What is the value of asking questions?

JC: That is a great question. I think that I've puzzled a lot on this and I think part of it is that it's very hard to filter a noisy and complicated and changing world. One of the things that became very clear to me in *How the Mighty Fall* was that the companies that fell kind of ceased to continually dig to try to understand the sources of their success and recognize that success is constantly a journey. You're always trying to better understand the sources of your success and the things that could imperil you. If you actually think that you have all those answers, you stop asking the questions. Well, what happens if, in fact, you were wrong about part of it? And then things start to go awry because you've lost that inquisitiveness, the will to try to truly understand. You may, in fact, put the accelerator on the wrong variables because you were wrong about why you were successful in the first place.

And so I think the sense of a relentless curiosity and a relentless quest to understand — even if you think you understand, and never really believe you fully understand — reflects the way that certain leaders navigated a world that was very foggy.

There's that classic phrase, I think it was Clausewitz, the concept of the "fog of war". If things are unfolding, it's easy, in retrospect, to say it's clear. But it's not clear at the moment. That's the thing that's so hard, to understand things at the moment. Well, if you have really great people around you to begin with and you ask them the right questions, you're probably more likely to at least have reasonably good answers than if you just assert the statement. Obviously you can get a genius but even geniuses can cease to be a genius, right? And it's a sort of an empirical observation about the Socratic nature of many of the best people that we've studied. They're great with questions. The funny thing is, when they didn't know the answer, they usually knew the right question to ask.

IBJ: Coming back to the book, you discuss what happens when the "What" replaces the "Why". Elaborate please?

JC: Think about it this way. You have a great enterprise that has a very strong set of values that's married to a very insightful strategy. That is then translated into a set of disciplined decisions, mechanisms, cultural practices and a variety of other things that really bring the strategy to life so that you can make good on it. And when you look at that chain, the great danger comes when you become dogmatic about what's at the lower level of that chain, when you become dogmatic about the practices, when you become dogmatic about the specific strategies, about the fact that we're successful because we do these things. The folks who originally came up with those things never really had any particular allegiance to those specific things. They had an allegiance to the understanding that led to doing those specific things.

The 10-minute turn (in which aircraft are emptied and moved away from the gate in ten minutes), if all it becomes is we're successful because we do the 10-minute turn, then that would be dogmatic. But Putnam and Kelleher (Southwest's President and CEO) had it. They understood the real "Why" behind the 10-minute and then the later 20-minute turn. They understood the link between the practice and the mechanism. "We understand why we do it. We do it because it gives us a day-to-day, actually hour-to-hour, mechanism of discipline that keeps us focused." That's number one.

Second, it's tied directly to cash flow and all businesses are about cash flow. But airplanes don't bring in cash if they're sitting on tarmacs. It goes all the way back to earlier in their history. They didn't have enough money for a fourth airplane, so they had to basically fill their schedule with only three when they would really have liked to have had four. The only way to do that was to turn the planes quicker than they would otherwise have done. And so they can go back and say the reason this is important, just think about what turns the engine that we have, the economic engine that we have. We can explain why we do the 20-minute or the 10-minute turns. There's a chain, there's a linkage, it ties into everything we do. The moment it becomes so dogmatic that we just do "these things", then that's when you become enormously imperiled because you become fixed to the specifics.

And just to zoom way out to a very big picture, Drucker was fond of talking about the [founding] of the United States of America. It's always been an interest of mine, as well as one of the observations he made, that ours was one of the first forms of government that didn't depend on a strong single leader. It had the Constitution. But the brilliance of the Constitution was the amendment mechanism. And it was the recognition that you needed this sacred document that had the mechanism in it. It was very concrete, but it had imbedded in it this mechanism to evolve, so that as you encountered new conditions, you could carefully evolve through the amendment mechanism and still have a living, breathing document. Well, if you just become dogmatic and said that we're going to keep the Constitution the way it was in 1787, because somehow that's sacred, rather than that it's the principles that are sacred, well you know what would happen. Well it's that same idea, when you are focusing on why do we do these things, why do we do these things? In most cases, the answers are that we should keep doing them because they still make sense and we can tell you why.

IBJ: Moving to Asia, what can North American managers learn from Asian companies?

JC: I'll give you two answers to that question, both of them short. The first is, in terms of what might be different over there, I don't know from the standpoint of not having done rigorous research on it. My answer is that I really don't know. I do know that we have a lot of students who find the ideas useful. Now that's not necessarily the same as doing a study on Japanese or Chinese companies.

The second answer to your question is that I think you can learn something from all these places. I'm reminded of the story that I actually put in *How the Mighty Fall.* It's an extremely important story, the one about the Brazilians visiting Sam Walton, to learn about discount retailing. He flips the whole thing around and then later he actually travels to Brazil. He's on his hands and knees measuring the widths of aisles and stuff. He gets thrown in jail because he's wandering around. His friends went and got him out. It was just a misunderstanding, but still, he was on his hands and knees behind cash registers measuring things. He was trying to learn everything he could from the Brazilians that might be helpful. I think if you asked Sam Walton, "Do you think there's something you can learn from anyone anywhere in the world?" his answer would be, "How many questions do I get?"

"Who" is Far More Important than "What"

IBJ: In your writing, you discuss how important it is to have "the right people on the bus". What do you mean and why is it important?

JC: I think that if I stand back and look across 20 years of doing these matched pair studies, there are two decades of doing this kind of work and about 7,000 years of combined corporate history through the different lenses of the databases that we looked at. As I zoom out from all of that, I say, "What has made the biggest impression on me in terms of an approach to any kind of organized performance, an approach to life that you just see it across, no matter what lens you put on, you see it?" It's this idea of the primacy of "Who" over "What". We see it in the research that we're doing on tumultuous environments. Because if you can't predict what the world is going to do, you can't possibly predict the "What". Then, your ultimate hedge against the "What" is to have the right people who can deal with whatever the world is going to throw at you. That is the great hedge against uncertainty.

And when you think about it, the great leaders were ones who really did focus first on getting people in place and then figure out what to do. It's what Lou Gerstner did at IBM. He built his team first and then forced everyone to think in a very disciplined way. Then they acted from there. And that's the case almost no matter what lens I look through. It's not this thing of taking care of your people or a team. It's the work first. First it's "Who", then everything else. And when I really think about that, it is also a life approach. Life is people, and your experiences with people, the people you fill your minutes and days and hours with. If your hours are filled with people who really aren't the right people to have in your life, it's really hard to have a great life. It's almost interesting to look at my own life. Almost every major mistake I've made has had, at its roots, a "Who" mistake that I've made. I think that we find that in almost every lens.

About the Author

Stephen Bernhut is editor of *Ivey Business Journal*. This article was originally published in the 2nd issue of *CEIBS Business Review* in 2009.

Index

D

www.ingramcontent.com/pod-product-compliance
Lightning Source LLC
LaVergne TN
LVHW011814200926
848484LV00005B/1199